Warman's®

Tools

FIELD GUIDE
2nd Edition

Clarence Blanchard

Values and Identification

Published by

Krause Publications, a division of F+W Media, Inc.
700 East State Street • Iola, WI 54990-0001
715-445-2214 • 888-457-2873
www.krausebooks.com

To order books or other products call toll-free 1-800-258-0929
or visit us online at www.krausebooks.com

ISBN-13: 978-1-4402-1437-0

ISBN-10: 1-4402-1437-9

Cover Design by Heidi Bittner-Zastrow
Designed by Wendy Wendt
Edited by Dan Brownell

Printed in the United States of America

Contents

Acknowledgments

The publisher wishes to thank Brown Auction Services for its valuable contribution to this book. Brown Auction Services and its semi-annual International Antique Tool Auction holds many world record antique tool prices and is the leader in the antique tool auction business.

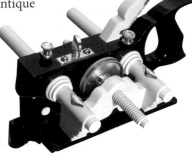

This Sandusky Tool Co. 1876 Centennial center-wheel plow plane sold for $114,400 at Brown's 24th International Antique Tool Auction, achieving the world record sale price for an antique tool.

For more information about International Antique Tool Auctions, contact:

Brown Auction Services
27 Fickett Road
Pownal, ME 04069
(800) 248-8114
www.finetoolj.com

Introduction

The first edition of the *Warman's Tools Field Guide* is now almost five years old. When we compiled our first price guide in 2003, the world record for a tool at auction was $32,900. That record has been broken several times and today the record is at $114,400. While it is not uncommon for a tool to sell for over $10,000 and sometimes for much more, a lot of changes in the pricing of old tools has occurred in the last few years. Let's take a look at some of those changes.

What tools are bringing the big money today? Two trends seem to be leading the way. First, patented items in general and planes in particular continue to bring the big bucks. If an item can be traced to a patent, it adds history and value. The second "hot" area is more general. Condition by itself can add or, for that matter, take away more value than any other single factor. It has become so important that collectors now use the term "dead mint" for those items in the top two percent of condition. To illustrate how big a role condition plays, in our Fall 2008 sale, a Stanley No. 1 plane in Good+ condition brought $880, while the same plane but in Fine+

sold for $2,090. That's a big difference, and had the plane in Fine+ been "dead mint," it could have brought much more.

Condition has become so important to collecting that I have added a chapter on evaluating the condition of Stanley tools. The manufacturing quality that Stanley maintained over many years sets a consistent base for comparing wear and tear from use or poor storage. Once you have an understanding of Stanley condition, it is easier to apply those principles to other tool groups, where the ratings can be more subjective.

Another area just now regaining interest is wooden planes and molders. Once the backbone of tool collecting, wooden planes have been a bit soft in the market for a while. Recently I have seen signs of reviving interest and an upward trend in prices. Complex molders and rare makers have just started to go up in value, and we could see some excitement over the next few years.

Not all areas of tool collecting have gone up in the last few years. The more common items, because of the Internet, are now more available worldwide. Before the Internet existed, we just never got a chance to buy many items, while today you can go online and get several opportunities a month to buy common tools. This global leveling of the market has driven down the price of poorer condition common items. That's the bad news. The good news is that in the last couple years supply seems to be falling and prices have leveled off and are gaining in some areas as well as for the better condition items.

With this edition, as with the first, all of the tools listed sold for the prices shown and have not been listed before. The prices listed are real, not estimates or opinions. Some of the tools shown are rare and expensive. Many other tools are more common and show up more often in sales and collections. Each year we get calls from people who have found items like the ones in this book. Sometimes we sell these items for good money; other times the finder makes them the centerpieces of their new collection. Either way, it all starts with an accurate identification and price guide.

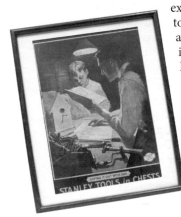

Focusing a Collection

So many tools exist in today's world that many tool collectors focus on one category. Some of the most popular categories to collect fall into the following general areas:

Function

Focusing on finding tools with a particular function is a popular way to specialize a collection. Some collectors seek out wooden planes, for example, while others hunt down wrenches, and some look only for hammers.

Craft or Trade

Others collect tools of a certain craft or trade: cooper, tinsmith, and wheelwright tools are popular examples of that type of collection. Many collectors in this group can be seen at demonstrations and craft fairs showing how their tools are used and demonstrating the methods used by the old-time trade person.

Personal Connection

Many collectors look for tools with certain names or connected to certain locations. Among these subcategories are particular family names or groups of names with historical connections, and hometowns, states, counties, or other special places. This group of collectors is quite large, with many having a "hometown" or "my name" collection in addition to their other areas of interest.

Company or Brand

Collecting tools made by a particular company or maker is common, too. Some makers have long since ceased production, while others are still making tools today. Stanley products make up one of the most sought-after company brands, and collections consisting of thousands of tools have been assembled around the Stanley name alone.

Patents

Yankee ingenuity thrived in the 19th century, and thousands of tool patents were issued. Some were successful, while others were never manufactured. A large group of collectors seek only patented tools. These collectors tend to be very specialized, and each addition to their collections must meet specific requirements. Some collect only one type of tool. Complete collections have been made up of only patented braces, for example, or just patented planes. Other collectors will only collect tools patented before a certain date. Still others are only interested in the patents of one company or individual.

Investment

Historically, tool collectors have not been primarily interested in making money from their hobby. As some early collections come to market, however, it is becoming obvious that tools can be a great investment. With an educated eye, miles of travel and hours of searching, some collectors have reaped excellent returns on their tool investments. As collecting continues to grow and monetary values increase, the investment side of the hobby must be considered. Clearly, with today's higher initial cost per tool, one must at least think about the long-term value of each purchase. Over the past few years, values have been steadily rising. All indications are that interest is strong and tool prices will continue to increase.

Values

What makes a tool valuable? A general answer is easy: quality. Most valuable tools will be of high quality. If a tool is well made from high-end materials, chances are it is worthy of investigation. Materials are easy to spot and well known to us all. Ebony is better than maple, and ivory trimmings are better than brass. Quality of manufacture is a bit harder to determine, but with a little effort you can learn what a better tool "feels" like. This will not tell you the value or keep you from missing tools that require special knowledge, but it should help you spot the gems.

To answer the value question in detail requires a great deal of knowledge that can take years to acquire. As with all collectible areas, three basic considerations are paramount among all determining factors: rarity, desirability, and condition. These factors must be considered first individually and then combined to determine value. Rarity and condition are generally fixed, while demand can change from time to time. All three factors combine to determine the importance of each item. Rarity sets the level of interest, demand controls the amount of interest, and condition determines how eagerly a collector will pursue any given item. Any single factor, when exceptional, can move a piece from obscurity to stardom. If all three factors come together on the same item, you have a superstar.

Like most antiques, tools make up a wide field that takes years of experience to master. Without the time or desire to acquire that level of knowledge, one can consult a price guide such as this.

This book is very helpful because all the tools listed show actual prices. That is important because the values listed are neither the price at which a tool was offered nor someone's idea of the value of a given tool, but represent what was actually paid for a particular tool.

While matching a tool to a listing can tell you what a particular tool sold for, it may not tell you the value of your example. The details are what determine the actual value. What this book can do is give you a general idea and maybe keep you from making a big mistake. Once you have found an item that appears to be the same as yours, you can use that information to determine how much more effort needs to be invested in determining the value of your item. For example, if you have a badly rusted handsaw and find the exact same saw listed for $25, it might not be worth further effort. On the other hand, if a similar saw lists for $3,000, your saw certainly has value and may be worth more study.

As you use this book, keep in mind that the listings are only guidelines. Detailed knowledge is required to determine a more precise value of any antique.

Condition Grades

The following criteria are used to determine condition grades of tools:

New: Tool is completely usable; metal is 100% with no rust; wood is as manufactured with smooth, sharp surfaces, no wear or repair.

Fine: Tool is completely usable; metal is 90%-100% and may have a trace of rust and some dark patina; wood 80% original or old finish, smooth surface and edges slightly rounded; minimal wear and no repair; maker's marks, if present, are clear and easily legible.

Good+: Tool is usable, but may need some tuning; metal is 75%-90% and may have light rust; wood has a well-patinated appearance, but may have minor surface stress, edges are good; wear is normal with minor or no repair; may have a few dings and scratches.

Good: Tool is usable, but may need significant tuning; metal is 50% to 75% and may have light rust or minor pitting; wood has pleasing patination but possibly some stains, and may have minor chips or shrinkage cracks; wear is normal to moderate and any repairs are minor but correct; represents average, as-found condition.

Good-: Tool is probably usable; metal 30%-50% with moderate rust and moderate pitting; wood is refinished or has warping, chips, minor splitting, and some patination, with prominent staining or discoloration; wear is moderate to heavy and repairs are correct; although the tool has problems, the general integrity is okay.

Fair: Tool is probably not usable; metal is 0%-30% with moderate to heavy rust and serious pitting; wood shows poor refinishing, or if original finish, shows extreme discoloration with warping, splits, major cracks, or large chunks missing; wear is excessive and repairs are major with improper or missing parts; normally not suitable to add to a collection, but may be good for parts.

Poor: Tool is not usable; metal has heavy rust and major pitting; wood has rot, rough surface, or glued splits; wear is excessive and tool is damaged and missing major parts; only useful for parts or raw materials for repair of tools in better condition.

Trends

As in all collecting areas, trends come and go in tool collecting. In the 1950s, blacksmith-made items were all the rage. Coopers' tools took the lead in the '60s, braces were hot in the '70s, and the wooden plane dominated in the '80s. In recent years the most significant trend has been the focus on condition, no matter what the tool.

Today tool collectors are more aware of condition than at any time in the past. Even an older common tool in "hardware-store new" shape has more value today than it did a few years ago. Rare Stanley planes that are "Mint in Box," for example, have sold for 8 to 12 times the price of a used example with no box. Today the fastest growing area of collecting is patented tools. Planes lead the way, with several selling for tens of thousands of dollars. Braces and wrenches are probably tied for second place.

Trends will change. The tool collecting hobby as it exists today is about 35 years old. Most areas of interest have become well established, and the factors determining value are known. So while fads may come and go, tool collecting is here to stay.

Building a Collection

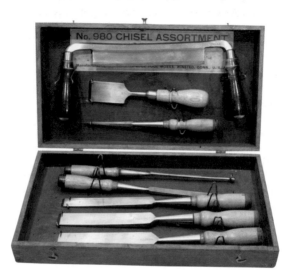

As you build your collection, learn all you can. Study your area of interest from top to bottom. Every dollar spent on a book and every minute spent reading will reward you tenfold. Once you have covered your primary interest, do not stop studying. Learn all you can about other types of tools. As you search for items in your area of interest, you will see many tools in related areas. Often your knowledge in another area will result in a purchase that can be converted into cash to build your collection.

As your hunt continues, keep in mind the importance of condition. For common tools, the only value may be exceptional condition. Remember, as many antique dealers have said, "Junk is always junk." Buy the best example you can afford in the best condition you can find.

The worst that can happen is that you will have a lot of fun, meet many great people and, with just a bit of luck, make a profit on your investment.

Collecting Stanley Tools

Collecting Stanley tools as a hobby is quite new. The first serious hobbyists started showing up in the early 1970s. But judging from the many old tool boxes and original shops I have visited over the years, the hobbyists of the 1970s were not the first Stanley collectors. Stanley Rule & Level began making rules and other tools in 1857. From day one, Stanley tools were of top quality and certainly the prize of any tradesman. Clearly, many early carpenters felt that adding one more Stanley item to their tool kit was a desirable goal even if they never used the tool. The modern tool collector identifies with that desire, and Stanley has become one of the leading collecting areas in old tools.

Since the early 1970s, Stanley tool collecting and tool collecting of all kinds has exploded. Many books, articles and guides have been published, and today a tremendous amount of information is available. Slowly the collecting focus has grown from wanting one of everything Stanley ever made to wanting specific items. With increased prices, Stanley collecting has changed. Collectors today are putting together smaller collections and choosing each new addition with greater care.

Pricing

The easiest way to think of values for Stanley tools—and for that matter, all antique tools—is to divide the pricing into categories based on condition. Each type of tool has a basic value. Some items are common and therefore lower in value;

others are rarer or in higher demand and therefore more valuable. Once you know the general value of an item, you need only consider its condition to determine its final value.

Pricing any collectible is not easy and can take considerable practice to master. For Stanley tools, however, it is somewhat easier than many other areas. Like coins, the various models can be listed and, in many cases, production periods have been established. Stanley tools can almost be collected by the model number. Once you know the value of a particular tool model, you can buy, sell, and collect by condition.

Type Studies

In Stanley tools, the number refers to the model of the tool. For example, No. 444 is a dovetail plane. The "type" is the year or range of years in which a tool with particular features was manufactured. Thanks to the effort of many people, several models of tools have been identified in detail and type studies have been written.

These type studies have been published in several books and offer extensive information on the design changes and improvements implemented over the years. In some cases, the studies go into great detail

and follow a tool from its early years until it was
dropped from production. Others studies are more
general or cover only a few types.

Type studies are based on collections and old
catalogs. The employees at Stanley did not have the
studies to go by and often used the parts that were
at hand. Therefore, it is not uncommon to find
even new condition tools that do not exactly meet
the conditions laid out in the study. Often, even
on a new plane in the box, a cutter or cap can be a

type or two behind or ahead depending on when supplies ran out. So unless you are trying to match a specific type, do not get too concerned about slight variations from the type study.

Type and Value

Type can affect value. Several general rules exist; they are not hard and fast, but can point a collector in the right direction. The earlier the type, the more likely a tool has a higher value. This especially applies to very early types that were made well before the tool model was established. Second, the shorter the time a particular type was manufactured, the more likely its value will be higher. Some types were manufactured for only a year or two and demand a higher value. Finally, the more significant the change, the more likely it impacts the value. Small changes, such as a new cutter logo, often have no effect, but larger changes, such as adding a cutter adjustment mechanism, nearly creates a new model.

Trademarks and Logos

From its earliest days, Stanley used trademarks and various logos to designate its products. So when it comes to dating Stanley tools, some of the most reliable information comes from dating these marks.

Research has accurately dated many of the marks, and today we know the range of dates when most marks were used. This information gives us an accurate, not-earlier-than date for the various marks and can be helpful in typing an item.

Stanley used a last-in, first-out inventory system, so occasionally an older part original to the tool can be found on a newer tool. This occurs most often with World War II types.

Trademarks were widely used in catalogs and advertising, and on original boxes. Some trademarks are the same as the cutter logos, but others are different. Many trademarks were used for long periods. The notched trademark is also a blade logo and has been used for the past few decades.

Following is a pictorial listing of some of the more commonly encountered logos and trademarks.

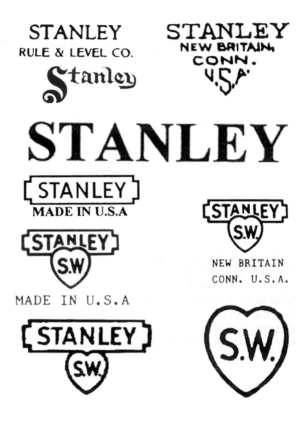

Condition

Condition may be the single most important factor in pricing Stanley tools. A plane may be the rarest model or the most eagerly sought-after type, but if its condition is not at least good, the value can be significantly reduced.

The *Fine Tool Journal Condition Classification for Antique Hand Tools* is included in this book. The chart lays out grades from poor to new. The current chart was last revised in 1991. If a new chart were to be developed for Stanley tools, it would have considerably more categories. In fact, it is likely that it would be more like the current grading system for collectible coins. In place of "MS" for "mint state" used by coin collectors, we might have "HS" for "hardware store state" with a number to quantify the HS state of each tool.

Some may think this is a bit overboard, but all you need to do is review a few major tool auctions to see how the tool-buying public is applying a detailed and concise buying strategy. Prices can die on good tools in poor shape but go through the roof for a not-so-rare tool that is "dead mint." For example, a few years ago, a Stanley 46 dado plane in the box sold for $4,600. A nicer plane could not have been found if you stood next to the Stanley production line in 1926 and had your choice. The finish had that frosty plating known as "Jack Frost plating." The plane just danced and sparkled like frost on a Maine window pane in January. Boxed Stanley 46 prices went through the roof for a few days but soon dropped back to the $600-$800 range that existed before this plane sold. The lesson here is not that one plane cannot change the market, but a collector will sometimes go an extra mile or ten for the very best.

A price of $4,600 for a Stanley 46 dado plane is over the top, so let's get back to the regular tool world. The standard for condition in tools has to be "hardware store new." The more a tool has been used or abused, the further it is from hardware store new, or fine condition. If you are pricing a tool at the top range, it should look like new. Phrases like "tools were meant to be used" or "looks good for its age" do not apply to tool collecting.

The *Fine Tool Journal Condition Chart* gives the basics for Stanley grading categories. Grades, like prices, should be thought of as ranges. The best fine condition tools command more money than the average fine condition tools. The collectors are already grading tools in great detail; auction results spell that out loud and clear. When you look at a prices-realized sheet and wonder why a certain item brought so much more or less than the average price for a particular model, more often than not the answer lies in condition.

To further help with understanding grading, the following photos review the same model tool in various grades. The first set shows a Stanley No. 4 bench plane—a common tool that represents many items in the Stanley line. The second set shows the Stanley No. 45 combination plane—another common tool that represents a number of different products that Stanley made. Both tools are common enough to give the reader the opportunity to find similar items for sale and practice grading.

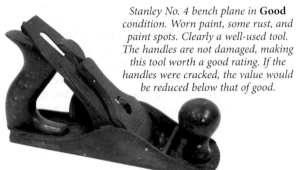

*Stanley No. 4 bench plane in **Good** condition. Worn paint, some rust, and paint spots. Clearly a well-used tool. The handles are not damaged, making this tool worth a good rating. If the handles were cracked, the value would be reduced below that of good.*

*Stanley No. 4 bench plane in **Good+** condition. This grade is for tools that have been taken care of and stored properly. The japanning will be 75% or better, and the polished surface should not be rusted or pitted. As with all grades, damaged wood and missing or broken parts reduce the value.*

*Stanley No. 4 bench plane in **Fine** condition. Finishes 90%
or better. Polished surfaces clean and bright or with uniform
patina. Damaged or missing parts considerably reduce the value
of tools in this condition. Original box adds value and should be
kept. See section on original boxes for more information.*

*Stanley No. 45 combination plane in **Fair-to-Good** condition. Plating worn and about 40%. Parts missing. The plane has a significant coat of rust. The wooden parts are OK, therefore not reducing the tool's value. If parts are damaged, a tool in this condition has little value to collectors.*

Stanley No. 45 combination plane in **Good** *condition. Plating about 70%. Wood OK. This is the typical condition of many planes. Note that this plane is missing a number of parts and a set of cutters. The missing items significantly reduce the tool's value but do not lower its condition rating.*

*Stanley No. 45 combination plane in **Good+** condition.
Plating about 90% and bright. Wood fine without damage.
A good, clean tool in better-than-average condition. This
plane's value is about one third that of the same plane with all
the parts and cutters. Add the original box in fine condition
and the value increases about 25%. For common tools, this
condition is often the minimum collectors will consider.*

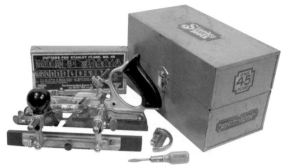

*Stanley No. 45 combination plane in **Fine** condition.
"Hardware store new" with little if any use. Plane is
complete with all the parts and the original metal box.
Although this plane is near mint, the minor wear on the box
keeps it from being in that desirable "dead mint" condition.*

Original Boxes

Collecting Stanley tools in their original boxes is
also popular. Stanley Works originated the idea of
the telescoping box for hardware in the early 1800s.
The telescoping box was a big success and was one
of the many innovations that made Stanley a major
player in the hardware business. A. Stanley & Co.
was selling its rules in the green telescoping box by
1857. Early boxes are rare, but it is assumed that

Stanley Rule & Level adapted the practice from A. Stanley & Co. and sold its products in boxes from the earliest days.

From early on, most Stanley tools came in two-piece boxes. Some of the earliest known boxes were made of wood with paste-on labels. In 1890, the green cardboard box became the primary type of container. In 1905, the familiar orange-tan (sweet-potato color) box was introduced with great fanfare. The 1905 catalog even had orange-colored pages to match the new box color. From 1905 into the 1950s, the orange box was the Stanley container of choice and as much a trademark for Stanley tools as the Sweet Hart or notched logos. The light tan color changed slightly over time. With the boxes of the 1950s, it became a bit more of a kraft color. Box labels changed slowly. It is not uncommon to find boxes with labels that are much earlier than the tool in the box.

In the late 1950s and early '60s, depending on the tool, a yellow box with reinforced corners was used. Also about that time, hang tags and pegboard displays were introduced. From the mid-1960s on, fewer boxes were used and plastic-sealed shelf and hang cards became the rule.

Box collecting is a specialty in itself. Some boxed items will sell for three or four times more than similar unboxed items. But not all boxed items bring the big bucks. For example, a No. 4 smooth plane with light use and a slightly worn box may not bring much of a premium over a fine condition No. 4. On the other hand, the No. 90 A rabbet plane, which is seldom found in fine condition, has sold for $10,000 in "dead mint" condition in a mint box, about three times the value of the tool alone.

Pricing boxes is not easy. Some general rules apply, but don't count on them for all the answers. First, box collecting is just that. No user planes in this group. If the boxed item you are pricing shows use and the box has wear to match, little premium should be added for the box.

Second, little boxes are more common than big boxes. Therefore, the bigger the box, the more likely the value will be higher. Again, this is only a general rule; great care must be taken in applying it.

Third, a box's age can add value. The early green boxes are generally hard to find. An early box in fine condition can add significantly to the value.

Fourth, rarity of the boxed tool is a major key to value. Generally, the rarer the unboxed item, the rarer the boxed item. There are exceptions. The No. 444 dovetail plane is rarer in well-used condition without the box than a good+ example in the box. Of course, the unboxed 444 is worth considerably less. In fact, the No. 444 dovetail plane in the box is the standard for that model and can be difficult to sell without the box.

Fifth, some items were never in an individual box. For example, rules were generally packed in boxes of six or more. The box was meant for shipping and then storage at the hardware store. When the box was empty, it was tossed out by the store clerk. These types of boxes seldom survived and can be quite rare.

Finally, like the 444 mentioned earlier, some common tools just seem to show up in the box. The No. 59 dowel jig and the No. 45 plane are a couple of examples. Both are quite common out of the box but are often found with the original boxes. For these tools, the box adds some value but not what it would for a rare item that seldom shows up boxed.

Advertising

As long as there have been tool manufacturers, there have been salesmen and advertisements to boost sales. The various posters, flyers, displays, and samples explain the advantages of the products so distributors, store owners, and the buying public are aware of how each tool can produce better quality work and make a job easier. While the advertising methods have changed over the years, the goal has not: to capture the attention of potential buyers, then convince them that the product featured can do the job better and for less money than the competitor's product.

The advertisements of the 1800s and earlier depended largely on printed advertising such as broadsides, signs, and flyers. They were generally fairly simple and limited in color and graphic design. Later, print ads became more sophisticated, featuring multiple colors and instantly recognizable logos. And of course, beginning in the 1900s, advertisers moved into the world of radio and television. And now, advertisers are taking advantage of the instant, world-wide access of the Internet. It will be interesting to see what forms of advertising will emerge next!

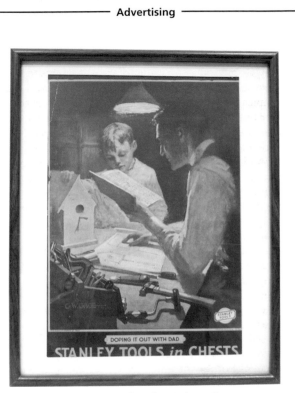

Advertising poster. "Stanley Tools in Chests, Doping It Out with Dad", 1922, father and son building a birdhouse, matted, framed, fine, $192.

Advertising poster. "Stanley Tools in Chests, Doping It Out with Dad", 1922, father and son building a birdhouse, matted, framed, fine....................................**$192**

Bridge set. Stanley, Sweet Hart, 1930s, two cigarette holders, four ash trays, one set in pink and gold, one set in green and black, good...**$60**

Clock. Stanley electric tools, probably 1930s, fine **$302**

Clock. Stanley Rule & Level, Weston Clock Co. alarm, good **$247**

Figure. Nearly life-size composition figure of the Stanley Man giving the thumbs-up w/ his right hand and holding tools in his left arm, some chipping, good................**$880**

Instructional display. Simonds handsaw, displays various steps in making a handsaw, six samples from blank piece of steel plate to finished saw, apple-wood handles shown from wood block to finished handle in seven stages, original display cards, corners damaged, various samples in nearly original condition, fine..**$440**

Letterhead. Sandusky Tool Co., c. 1910, shows plant and various tools, framed, fine...**$198**

Level sample kits. Stanley, display models and sample for wood and aluminum levels, cut section in display box, folding section in wood w/ list of sizes and features, two 24" cases each contain two aluminum level samples, one sample does not have vials installed, fine.........**$154**

Glass tray. Keen Kutter, 1" deep, logo reversed on backside, "Made in Germany", good+, $99.

Manufacturing display. Stanley hammers, seven samples from billet to finished hammer, includes "Making Stanley Hammers" booklet w/ slides, fine **$286**

Model plow. W.A. Camfield, c. 1887, single bottom, horse drawn, handles broken, includes studio card photo and handwritten note documenting origin, good+ **$60**

Point-of-sale display. Stanley screwdrivers, metal folding rack holds 12 drivers, paper label on front, screwdrivers not as early as rack, store tag from American Hardware and Equipment Co., Charlotte, N.C., fine, $187.

Point-of-sale display. Disston saws, round rack holds 15 handsaws, minor rust spots, one piece of wood missing from plywood ring, finish about 90%, good **$330**

Point-of-sale display. Sargent VBM No. 9 plane w/cutaway side, Shaw patent, open side shows frog bedding, some pitting, good.................................... **$220**

Point-of-sale display. Stanley door latch, Sweet Hart brass tag, works from both sides, some dings, good **$198**

Point-of-sale display. Stanley Works ball-bearing butts No. BB239A, early Sweet Hart brass tag on outside, hinged to open, celluloid nameplate on inside, good+, $170.

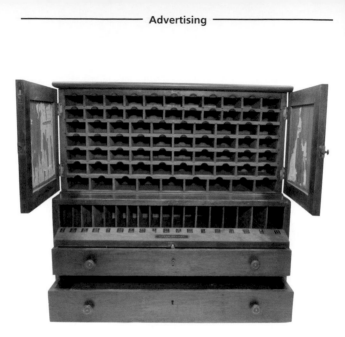

Point-of-sale display. Cleveland twist drill, walnut step-back cabinet, 75 cubbyholes in top section, two drawers and dropdown front w/ 18 cubbies in bottom section, traces of paper labels for drill size, good+, $825.

Point-of-sale display. Luther Dimogrit tool grinders, cast iron, diamond trademark on top of globe, japanning 96%, includes bench-model hand-crank grinder, fine, $138.

*Point-of-sale display.
Stanley Happy
Carpenters window
display, two-piece
main section, four
freestanding sections,
each die-cut piece
stands up and is
designed to hold
separate tool, fine,
$3,850.*

Point-of-sale display. Stanley rules, c. 1915, zigzag countertop display w/ black mirror, lithographed metal, green and gold, wood base, finish about 96%, good+ **$1,540**

Point-of-sale display. Eleven new Stanley No. 6386 push-pull tape rules, light wear on box, one corner torn, fine **$385**

Point-of-sale display. Stanley jersey vise stand, refinished w/ new wood, five vises, fine **$522**

Point-of-sale display. Starrett countertop case, about 20 tools displayed behind glass, three clips empty, wood, locking door in back, key, fine **$220**

Point-of-sale display. Starrett, wall case w/ about 39 new tools, designed to hang on hardware store wall, 21" by 33", oak, fine **$770**

Poster. Nicholson files, various types and descriptions, heavy canvas, metal edges top and bottom, good+ **$82**

Point-of-sale display. Stanley screwdrivers, metal folding rack holds 12 drivers, paper label on front, screwdrivers not as early as rack, store tag from American Hardware and Equipment Co., Charlotte, N.C., fine **$187**

Point-of-sale display. Stanley Legend PowerLock, molded display, carpenter holding visor of hat and offering 16 PowerLocks, multicolored, 19" by 28", fine **$522**

Point-of-sale display. Stanley Legend PowerLock, molded display, carpenter holding visor of hat and offering 16 PowerLocks, multicolored, 19" by 28", fine, $522.

Point-of-sale display. Stanley Works ball-bearing butts No. BB239A, early Sweet Hart brass tag on outside, hinged to open, celluloid nameplate on inside, good+ **$170**

Salesman's sample. Quick release for buggies, allows horse to be disconnected from carriage while still harnessed, fine.. **$247**

Point-of-sale display. Starrett saw blades, 1970s or '80s, dozens of types and sizes, label on back indicates may have been custom made, fine, $192.

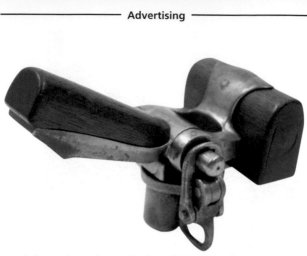

Salesman's sample. Quick release for buggies, allows horse to be disconnected from carriage while still harnessed, fine, $247.

Salesman's sample. Anchor Buggy Co., Cincinnati, Ohio, wagon fifth wheel, patented, connects axle and horse to wagon w/ pivoting device, good **$160**

Salesman's sample. Stanley No. 5 1/4 plane for Ready Edge blades, Sweet Hart, side of plane cut away to show Ready Edge blade in plane, "Ready Edge" mark on blade, new, previously Ballintine and Curry collections, fine **$1,100**

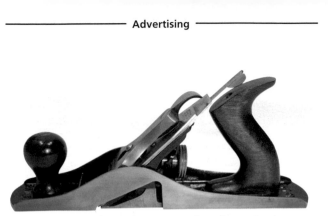

Salesman's sample. Stanley No. 5 1/4 plane for Ready Edge blades, Sweet Hart, side of plane cut away to show Ready Edge blade in plane, "Ready Edge" mark on blade, new, previously Ballintine and Curry collections, fine, $1,100.

Salesman's sample. Carborundum stones, full roll of nine plus two extras, unused, full Indian chief logo on most, fine **$165**

Salesman's sample. True Temper, pitchfork, three tines, 30", original finish 98%, original tine protector and canvas case, fine **$495**

Sign. "Carriage Shop, J.H. Carville, Farmington, Maine," age unknown, hand painted on board, good+
.... **$440**

Sign. Estwing Hatchets, plastic composition in shape of a hatchet, wall hanger, 37", fine **$27**

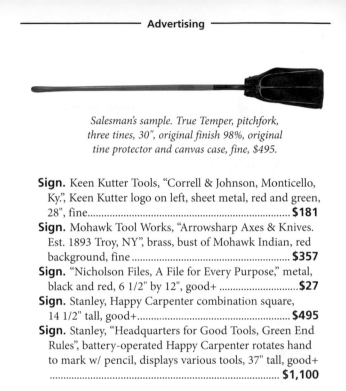

Salesman's sample. True Temper, pitchfork, three tines, 30", original finish 98%, original tine protector and canvas case, fine, $495.

Sign. Keen Kutter Tools, "Correll & Johnson, Monticello, Ky.", Keen Kutter logo on left, sheet metal, red and green, 28", fine...**$181**

Sign. Mohawk Tool Works, "Arrowsharp Axes & Knives. Est. 1893 Troy, NY", brass, bust of Mohawk Indian, red background, fine **$357**

Sign. "Nicholson Files, A File for Every Purpose," metal, black and red, 6 1/2" by 12", good+ **$27**

Sign. Stanley, Happy Carpenter combination square, 14 1/2" tall, good+...**$495**

Sign. Stanley, "Headquarters for Good Tools, Green End Rules", battery-operated Happy Carpenter rotates hand to mark w/ pencil, displays various tools, 37" tall, good+ **$1,100**

Salesman's sample. Joyce Cridland Co., Dayton, Ohio, paperweight house jack, working model, hollow-base casting, plating 95% and bright, fine, $358.

Salesman's sample. Stump and rock puller, ratchet mechanism, 12", painted black, good, $105.

Trade token. John Wilkinson Iron Master,
1791 halfpenny, man working at anvil on one
side, bust of Wilkinson on other, good, $50.

Books & Catalogs

An interesting adjunct to the collecting of tools themselves is the gathering of old books, catalogs, magazines, manuals and photos that help tell the story of tools. Since there are so many types of tools to collect, there is obviously a huge volume of published material to choose from. As you will see, some old literature can sell for a few dollars, with rarer items bringing several hundred.

Book. Complete Diderot Plates, EAIA reprint, 1,146 pages, half leather bound, French text, covers 18th century, fine **$88**

Book. Patented Transitional & Metallic Planes in America, Vols. 1 and 2, Roger Smith, fine **$154**

Book. Stanley Tools Big Book, John Walter, 865 pages, hard cover, dust cover, fine........................**$203**

Book. Stanley Tools Big Book, 1996 edition, 885 pages, good+ **$220**

Catalog. Akron Eclipse spirit level, c. 1920, 15 pages, paper cover, distributed by John S. Fray Co., fine......**$27**

Catalog. Leonard Bailey & Co., January 1883, 12 pages, foldout, patented adjustable bench planes, minor edge roughness, fine **$165**

Catalog. Leonard Bailey & Co., January 1883, 12 pages, foldout, full Victor line, original mailing envelope, fine
....**$132**

Catalog. Bigelow and Dowse Co., 1901, 549 pages, hard cover, leather corners and binding, some wear on covers, good+ **$93**

Catalog. Buck Bros., London-style carving tools, 1908, four pages, foldout, lists full line of carving tools from No. 1 to No. 44 in 11 sizes, stag logo and cut of factory on front, fine...**$27**

Catalog. Emerson and Fisher Hardware No. 24, St. John, New Brunswick, 243+ pages, color ads including Stanley Four Square, good+ **$93**

Catalog. Hammacher, Schlemmer & Co. No. 547, 320 pages, paper cover, tools, benches, hardware, from desk of Stanley superintendent E.A. Schade, binding torn, good+...**$110**

Catalog. P. Lowentraut Manufacturing Co., 1915 date stamped in corner, 52 pages, minor edge damage on corners, good+ **$209**

Catalog. Millers Falls Tools dealer catalog No. 39, 195 pages, color pictures of various point-of-sale displays, clean covers, good+ **$132**

Catalog. Montgomery & Co. Tools, New York, pre-1900, 700 pages, hard cover, good **$110**

Catalog. North Brothers Manufacturing Co., 1923, 252 pages, hard cover, foldout, Yankee tools, ice-cream freezers, color prints of point-of-sale displays, from A. Stowell at Stanley plant, fine.......................................**$385**

Catalog. Russell & Erwin Manufacturing Co. Vol. VIII, 1894, Richard Ryan, 926 pages, hard cover, full line for hardware trade, fine..**$247**

Catalog. Sandusky Tool Co., 1879, eight pages, foldout, framed, horse-drawn rake, roller, and corn cultivator, fine **$50**

Catalog. Stanley, January 1865, 39 pages, paper cover, good+..**$385**

Catalog. Stanley, January 1866, 52 pages, paper cover, fine **$577**

Catalog. Stanley, 1879, 66 pages, hard cover, fine **$825**

Catalog. Stanley, Jan. 1, 1881, 12 pages, foldout, bench plane, good..**$88**

Catalog. Stanley, Jan. 1, 1887, 16 pages, foldout, pale blue, good+ **$220**

Catalog. Stanley, 1888, 65 pages, hard cover, fine
....**$825**

Catalog. Stanley dealer's catalog No. 39, 1908, 69 pages plus index and package-size listing, loose cover, couple of first pages missing, good...**$55**

Catalog. Stanley dealer's catalog No. 102, 1909, 117 pages, etchings of full line of tools, binding loose, good **$27**

Catalog. Stanley pocket catalog, 1914, 34 pages, French text, nearly full line, toolbox of world globe logo on back, cover torn and loose, good..................................**$27**

Catalog. Stanley Four Square, 1923, 24 pages, two colors, fine **$192**

Catalog. Stanley No. 50, 1940, 56 pages, many tools marked w/ airplane to indicate they meet government specifications, some dirt but intact, good **$50**

Catalog. Stanley dealer's catalog No. 139, March 15, 1941, 242 pages, loose-leaf binder, notes and paste-in addition show tools coming and going as war progressed, clean, fine...**$77**

Catalog. Stanley No. 34S, 1953, 200 pages, Spanish text, 5 1/2" by 8 1/2", minor edge roughness, fine **$137**

Catalog. Union No. 7, 1921, 26 pages, iron and wood planes, fine..**$165**

Catalog. A.J. Wilkinson & Co., possibly 1880s, 117 pages, soft cover, good+...**$214**

Catalog. George Worthington Co., Cleveland, Ohio, 1930, 1,447 pages, good+..**$132**

Magazines. Nine issues of *Old Time New England*, missing July 1928 issue, but includes an extra copy of January 1928, Henry C. Mercer's classic Mercer's Ancient Carpenters' Tools first appeared in the pages of this magazine, rare, good condition **$28**

Printing plate. I.&D. Smallwood, copper, probably used in printing catalog, fine...**$33**

Magazines. Nine issues of Old Time New England, missing July 1928 issue, but includes an extra copy of January 1928, Henry C. Mercer's classic Mercer's Ancient Carpenters' Tools first appeared in the pages of this magazine, rare, good condition, $28.

Braces & Bits

A brace is a form of hand-held boring device fitted with a metal corkscrew-shaped "bit" that actually does the drilling. According to tool authority Ronald Barlow, the Chinese are credited with inventing the double-crank brace about 100 A.D. It appears the brace did not become available in Europe until much later—about the 15th century.

The earliest braces were crafted of fine hardwood with only the bit being made of metal. By the 18th century, some better braces were trimmed with brass reinforcing plates to make them stronger. The next major step in development came in 1850 when Mr. William Marples of Sheffield, England, developed his "ultimate" brace, equipped with a cast-brass frame and exotic hardwood infill. This became known as the "Ultimatum" type. About this same time, a number of all-metal braces were produced in the United States. Eventually, the all-metal version replaced the wood infill type and by the turn of the 20th century, it had become the world standard.

Blacksmith's brace press. Handwrought, early, wall mounted, swings to adjust for distance from wall, screw advances to apply pressure on brace, good+............ **$137**

Brace. B. Darling, patented, Oct. 20, 1868, lever arm pulls up chuck and locks bit in place, holes in brace frame secure lever, good+, $660.

Brace. C.H. Amidon patent, May 13, 1884, corner brace has free pivoting chuck section, brass pad on chuck allows direct pressure at point of action, good........ **$176**

Brace. Possibly ash, early, 22" plus bit, sweep 8", good+ **$99**

Brace. Bauwens, crank tie-wire twister and brace for securing wires around shipping crates, patented, Oct. 28, 1923, and Jan. 23, 1940, includes patent drawings and user information from company, fine..................**$82**

Brace. Bennett & Bloedel, patented, Oct. 10, 1905, corner brace, detachable handle, polished, good+ **$242**

Brace. Booth & Mills, probably maple, plated, lignum pad, tight check in pad, good **$462**

Brace. J. Bruford & Co., beech, plated, ebony pad, slide chuck, good+ **$198**

Brace. Joseph Cooper patent, beech, plated, brass stem, rosewood pad, one plating screw missing, good **$187**

Brace. Down Brothers, London, gunmetal, possibly military and medical, marked w/ British broad arrow, fine **$105**

Brace. Greenleaf Stackpole patent, March 18, 1867, brass chuck shell w/ spiral groove to lock jaws to bit, good **$242**

Brace. Horton No. 2528, Sheffield, registered, Nov. 8, 1850, brass frame and pad, rosewood handle, spring chuck, good, $578.

Framed brace. William Marples, c. 1872, ebony, ivory ring, fine+, $385.

Brace. Dake, patented, Sept. 16, 1884, geared mechanism rotates chuck as grip is turned, spiral-locking device for changing from grip mode to standard brace mode, possibly unique, good, $3,080.

Brace. Horton No. 2528, Sheffield, registered, Nov. 8, 1850, brass frame and pad, rosewood handle, spring chuck, good+ **$990**

Brace. Iosh, dated 1837, Northern European, replaced clothespin pod, some worm, good **$198**

Brace. Probably maple, eight pods, spring clip locks pods in place, good+ **$302**

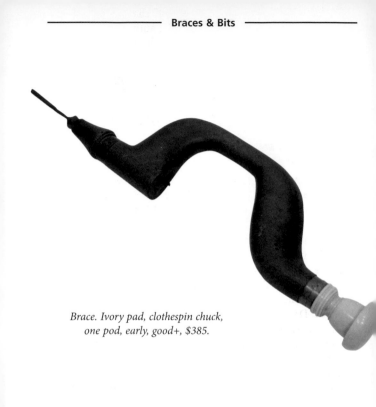

*Brace. Ivory pad, clothespin chuck,
one pod, early, good+, $385.*

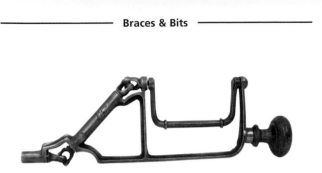

Brace. A.C. Derlon patent, Aug. 23, 1892, marked "F.G. 1", cast-iron frame w/ T-shaped cross section, enclosed crank, universal joints drive chuck, good, $412.

Brace. William Marples, ultimatum, brass frame, beech infill, ivory ring in pad, good+ **$385**

Brace. Stephen McClellan patent, June 8 and 28, 1897, corner brace, detachable handle, offset crank, shoulder pad, frame plating 90% and bright, good+ **$137**

Brace. Dake, patented, Sept. 16, 1884, geared mechanism rotates chuck as grip is turned, spiral-locking device for changing from grip mode to standard brace mode, possibly unique, good **$3,080**

Brace. A.C. Derlon patent, Aug. 23, 1892, marked "F.G. 1", cast-iron frame w/ T-shaped cross section, enclosed crank, universal joints drive chuck, good................. **$412**

Brace. Northern European, flat-tang chuck, file decorated, early, good...**$33**

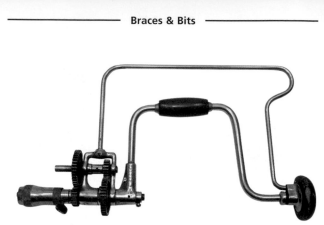

Brace. John H. Morrison, patented, Feb. 1, 1898, multispeed, double frame, multiple brass gears, plating 95%, good+, $522.

Brace. H. Perkins patent, Nov. 1, 1853, heavy cast-iron frame, sliding bar engages bit, light pitting, good... **$275**

Brace. Pexto, probably Stanley made, aluminum handle, sweep 14", polished, fine...**$60**

Brace. Pilkington, Pedigor & Storr, beech, brass stem, ebony head, lever chuck, all proper marks, good+
....**$1,760**

Brace. C.&T. Pilkington, beech, brass stem, ebony pad, heavy brass plates, crack at top of crank, good **$660**

Brace. Scandinavian, carved cranks fitted to grip, one pod, good+...**$176**

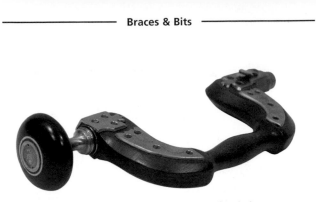

Brace. Pilkington, Pedigor & Storr, beech, brass stem, ebony head, ivory ring, lever chuck, all proper marks, even patina on brass, good, $1,265.

Brace. John H. Morrison, patented, Feb. 1, 1898, multispeed, double frame, multiple brass gears, plating 95%, good+ **$522**

Brace. Stanley No. 923A, aluminum handles, 8", original box, fine+ **$467**

Brace. Pilkington, Pedigor & Storr, beech, brass stem, ebony head, ivory ring, lever chuck, all proper marks, even patina on brass, good **$1,265**

Brace and bits. Millers Falls No. 602, corner brace, set of 13 Snell Star bits, patented, May 30, 1883, wood box, good and better **$220**

*Brace and bits. Jennings & Griffin Manufacturing Co.
No. 51B, six augers, screwdriver, plating 90%, original
wood box, labels 97% and fully readable, good, $176.*

Brace and bits. Jennings & Griffin Manufacturing Co.
No. 51B, six augers, screwdriver, plating 90%, original
wood box, labels 97% and fully readable, good....... **$176**

Brace. Norwegian, early, brass and wrought iron, flat tang, brass pad and grip decorated w/ rope turnings, heart thumbscrew locks bit, good+, $440.

Brace. Patented, chuck tilts sideways to install bit and tilts back to secure bit in spring-clip jaws, good+, $143.

Brace. Henry W. Porter patent, June 9, 1857, West Earl, Lancaster County, Pa., beech brace, rosewood pad, first U.S. patent for a ratcheting brace, removable iron shaft runs from top crank to bottom crank, clip top and bottom holds shaft in place, lever alongside lower crank controls ratchet direction, slip-ring chuck, little use, fine, $17,050.

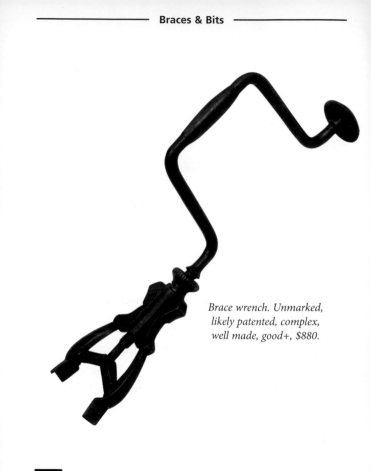

Brace wrench. Unmarked, likely patented, complex, well made, good+, $880.

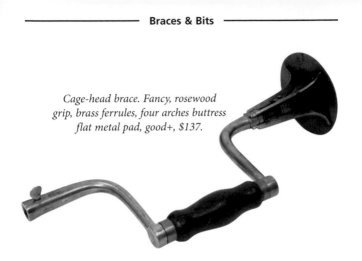

Cage-head brace. Fancy, rosewood grip, brass ferrules, four arches buttress flat metal pad, good+, $137.

Cage-head brace. Four posts, screw chuck, pad diameter 5 1/4", sweep 1", good..................................**$203**
Cage-head brace. Handwrought, four posts, file decoration on chuck, no thumbscrew, good...............**$66**
Cage-head brace. Handwrought, four poles, 19 1/2", sweep 8", good...**$77**
Cage-head brace. Norwegian, two poles, bit locked w/ spring clip, heavy wood pad, good...........................**$110**
Chair maker's brace. Probably 18th century, iron plates on lower crank and ferrule, good.................................**$27**

Chair maker's brace. One pod, spoon bit, sweep 6", chip on side of pad, good..**$38**

Chair maker's brace. Three pods, spoon bits, larger than typical, good+..**$236**

Chair maker's breast plate. Iron, worn around chest, pad of bit brace rests in slot on plate to free up one hand to hold work, good **$50**

Compendium tool. Ten bits, folding, good tip on corkscrew, good..**$154**

Framed brace. Cast iron, wood knob and handle, 11", good **$93**

Framed brace. Colquhoun & Cauman, ebony, brass frame, lever-locking chuck, brass button in pad, good+ **$605**

Framed brace. James Howarth, ebony, brass frame, solid adjustment, grip has tight check, good+ **$412**

Framed brace. H.G. Long & Co., ebony, ivory ring, tight joints, good+..**$302**

Framed brace. William Marples, c. 1860, ebony, transitional type, full ivory ring, brass pinged to blur references to Royal Arms and Letters patent, previously Tom Witte collection, good+ **$412**

Framed brace. William Marples, c. 1872, ebony, ivory ring, fine+ **$385**

Framed brace. William Marples, beech, full ivory ring, chuck engraved "W. Langford, Pattern Maker" in script, previously Tom Witte collection, good+ **$632**

Framed brace. Pilkington, Pedigor & Co., patented, beech body, brass stem, ebony pad, heavy brass plates, spring chuck, good, $880.

Framed brace. William Marples, ebony, perfect ivory ring, fine...**$522**

Framed brace. William Marples Ultimatum, beech infill, ivory ring, couple of checks in grip and ring, good **$275**

Framed brace. William Marples Ultimatum, ebony infill, ivory ring, check in pad, good........................**$297**

Framed brace. William Marples Ultimatum, ebony infill, ivory ring, check in pad, fine...........................**$495**

Framed brace. T. Tillotson & Co., Sheffield, Pilkington type, beech, ebony pad, button pad chuck, previously Tom Witte collection, good+ **$990**

French chair maker's brace. Original spoon bit, brass chuck plates, good..**$115**

Joist auger. Millers Falls No. 52, polished, repainted, fine **$215**

Pod auger. Possibly 18th century, burl, bit from a file, good **$126**

Pod auger. Natural tree-limb handle, end of handle appears to be a dog's face, good+ **$110**

Pod augers. Graduated set of six, 5/16" to 5/8", turned matching handles, good+ **$198**

Surgeon's brace. Mauer & Meltzer, London, 11" including bit, sweep 3 1/2", plating 65%, good........**$165**

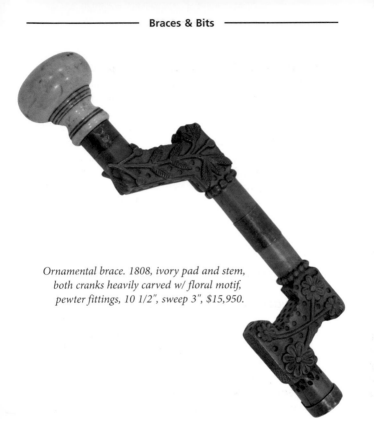

*Ornamental brace. 1808, ivory pad and stem,
both cranks heavily carved w/ floral motif,
pewter fittings, 10 1/2", sweep 3", $15,950.*

Piano maker's brace. Unmarked, Keene, N.H., rosewood, steel shell, two-jaw chuck, 11", sweep 3", fine, $385.

Surgeon's brace. Detached spiral-carved pad, fluted grip, four bits, five other tools, fitted velvet-lined walnut case w/ glass top, good+ **$1,980**

Surgeon's brace. Stanley, one bit, plating 95%, fine **$60**

T auger bit. 6/8 size, whale-bone handle, good+ **$198**

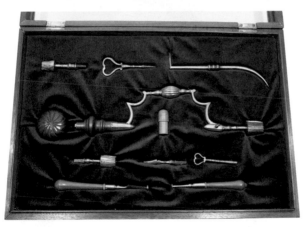

Surgeon's brace. Detached spiral-carved pad, fluted grip, four bits, five other tools, fitted velvet-lined walnut case w/ glass top, good+, $1,980.

Sims framed brace. Ward, early heavy frame, three saw label screws for bolts, much original finish, fine, $2,970.

Surgeon's brace. Delicate lines, 10 1/2", sweep 3 1/2", some original finish, good+, $105.

Tool handle and bits. Bagshaw & Field, rosewood handle marked but weak, 16 bits, several marked, fitted box, couple of chips on handle, good **$165**

Wagon maker's brace. Possibly elm, handwrought chuck and pad bolt, almost 23", sweep 10", old sheet-plate repairs to chuck, good **$82**

Wagon maker's brace. Possibly elm, thumbscrew chuck, one pod, iron ferrule, 19", sweep 15", good....**$82**

Washer-cutting brace. Double sliding cutter heads can be set along lower crank for washers of various diameters, good+ **$132**

Washer-cutting brace. I.B. Heysinger, patented, Oct. 16, 1883, adjustable cutters, japanning worn, good, $105.

Washer-cutting brace. I.B. Heysinger, patented, Oct. 16, 1883, adjustable cutters, japanning worn, good **$105**

Wooden brace. 18th century, one pod w/ iron ring, 16 1/2", sweep 7", good+ **$176**

Wooden brace. 18th century, thumbscrew locking pod, old red paint, hammered brass ferrule on pod, good+ **$220**

Wooden brace. Dutch, elm, 10", sweep 4", good **$60**

Wooden brace. Early, fluted cranks, half-round sweep at cranks, 15", sweep 10", many worm holes, good **$71**

Wooden brace. European, early, clothespin pod, 19", hand-forged spoon bit, good **$137**

Wooden brace. Fitted w/ tapered reamer made from a file, 20", sweep 11", good **$55**

Wooden brace. Possibly maple, carved from single burl, "EES" owner's mark, additional pod fits but not original to brace, some minor checking, good+ **$209**

Wooden brace. Possibly Northern European, three screw pods, 13", sweep 6", good+ **$264**

Wooden brace. Wing nut on top of chuck closes steel jaws around bit, good+ **$99**

Wooden brace. Young, Cincinnati, Ohio, tapered chuck, three chair maker's pods, only one pod fits brace, 16" w/o pod, sweep 10", good **$231**

Wooden brace. Five chair maker's pods, chuck is single piece of bone threaded to receive pods, probably unique, good+, $660.

Drills

Drills also have ancient origins and are somewhat related to braces, except that drills are typically operated with gears, rather than a crank, and tend to have more specialized uses. Also, more modern drills can be operated with one hand.

Probably the earliest type of drill is the bow drill, which has probably been around for some 10,000 years. This style required a bow-shaped section that was pulled back and forth rapidly by hand to power the vertical drill tool. By Roman times, pump drills had been developed that could be operated with one hand. Much later came breast drills that were fitted at the top with a curved brace against which the user could lean with his chest, thus enabling him to have the full force of his body to steady and push the drill.

It wasn't until the later 19th century that the more modern push-style drill was developed that eventually developed the double-spiral grooves on the shaft for easier hand-pumping action. Although still used well into the 20th century, most people now depend on easy-to-use electric power models.

Bench drill press. Goodell-Pratt Co., holds breast drill, screws to bench w/ tripod base, auto advance, fine **$385**

Pistol-grip hand drill. Stanley No. 610, second Sweet Hart, type 1, no bit caddy, hand and gear wheel redesigned before production began, possibly unique, japanning and paint 95%, fine, $770.

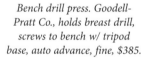

Bench drill press. Goodell-Pratt Co., holds breast drill, screws to bench w/ tripod base, auto advance, fine, $385.

Bow drill. Boxwood handle, brass trimmings, dark wood spool, fine.. **$357**

Bow drill. Napoleon Erlandsen No. 8, New York City, rosewood, brass, ivory spool, fine **$797**

Bow drill and bow. Buck, maker mark around brass ring hard to read, ebony, one chip in spool, stress crack in handle, good.. **$247**

Bow drill and bow. Buck, ebony spool and handle, steel bow, brass fittings, marks readable but faint, good **$253**

Bow drill and bow. Ebony, brass, wood bow, probably manufactured, good+ **$165**

Breast auger. Possibly 18th century, 27", good **$66**

Breast drill. A.J.W. & Co. No. 3, rosewood handles, large top-of-the-line drill, gears and body painted green, paint 90%, rest of metal plated and bright, good+............ **$137**

Drill. Rusby patent, complete, proper handles, breast pad, finishes about 95%, fine **$132**

Fly-ball drill. D.R. patent A, pump handle, large brass balls keep drill spinning, good+ **$302**

Frame drill. Brass, cast-iron gears, ogee wings support pad, missing chuck screw, good.................................. **$143**

Frame drill. Brass, large mushroom pad, brass and steel gears, 12", good **$93**

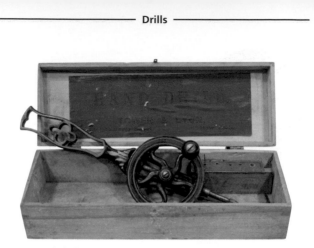

Hand drill. Tower & Lyon, Whitney patent, May 4, 1886, black japanning w/ red and gold decoration, finish about 98%, original box, good inside label, fine, $1,155.

Frame drill. Steel gears, cranks, and handle, wood knob and handle, good+ **$88**

Hand drill. Tower & Lyon, Whitney patent, May 4, 1886, black japanning w/ red and gold decoration, finish about 98%, original box, good inside label, fine

.... **$1,155**

Hollow auger. Swan No. 0001, improved universal, original instructions, original wood box, label faint, fine

.... **$132**

Lens drill for eyeglasses. For drilling screw holes in lens, bench mounted, hand cranked, gold and black finishes 95%, includes set of old glasses for demonstrating drill, fine, $126.

Jeweler's bow drill and bow. Bone spool and handle, drill 6", wood box w/ some chip carving, good+ **$143**

Lens drill for eyeglasses. For drilling screw holes in lens, bench mounted, hand cranked, gold and black finishes 95%, includes set of old glasses for demonstrating drill, fine **$126**

Pistol-grip hand drill. Stanley No. 610, Sweet Hart, finish 60%, good **$220**

Pistol-grip hand drill. Stanley No. 610, Sweet Hart, caddy cover missing, finish 70%, good..................... **$198**

Pistol-grip hand drill. Stanley No. 610, second Sweet Hart, type 1, no bit caddy, hand and gear wheel redesigned before production began, possibly unique, japanning and paint 95%, fine **$770**

Pistol-grip hand drill. Stanley No. 610, Sweet Hart, finish 80%, good **$286**

Pull-chain drill. Mc.G. S. Ltd., Glasgow trademark gyro, rosewood handle on chain, caddy under breast pad, works but return spring slow, good............................**$77**

Pump drill. Brass ball, copper shaft, early, good....... **$159**

Pump drill. Goodell Pratt, two-handed, plating 95% and bright, orange paint on breast pad about 93%, fine

.... **$286**

Pump drill. Handwrought decorated iron, weight has floral casting, four tapered sides on chuck, holds an extension, good+.. **$110**

Pump drill. Handwrought flywheel, wood pump, leather straps, 30", good..**$66**

Edged Tools

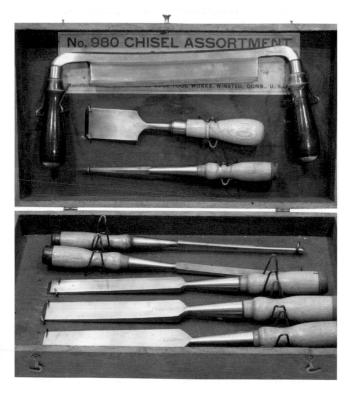

This section includes a variety of tools that rely on sharpened edges to produce the desired results. The most common tool of this type is the ax, with its smaller cousin, the hatchet. Narrowbladed hand adzes are used to chip out narrow grooves in wood, as are various types of chisels and draw knives. Draw knives have long, narrow, and gently curved metal blades with wooden angled handles at the ends. They derive their name from the fact that the user "drew" or pulled them towards his body when using them for trimming work on narrow boards or spindles.

In prehistoric times, the earliest axes were chipped from stone and eventually were tied to wooden handles. Metal heads were developed during the Bronze Age, and just a few years ago, the earliest such tool was discovered among the objects belonging to the famous "Ice Man," whose body was discovered near the border of Austria and Italy. This discovery prompted scientists to push the start of the Bronze Age back at least 1,000 years.

Eventually iron became the material of choice for all such tools, and handwrought axes of all types were made into the early 19th century. There are many varieties of axes, with the most common being those used to fell or hew trees, but special styles evolved into battle axes, mortising axes, and the gruesome beheading axes. One variety, called the "goosewing ax," gets its name from the long, gently curved wing-like blade.

The first American factory for mass-producing handwrought axes was opened in the 1820s. By the mid- 19th century, more refined machine-made axes and hatchets gradually replaced the handcrafted types, and quality steel put an end to the ancient iron ax.

Bowl adze. French, handwrought, two dished-out areas on backside, old handle, 8″, good+, $176.

Ax. Bronze Age, shaft handle, rounded decoration along top of handle shank, 4", good+ **$105**

Ax. Bronze Age, Celtic, 8th century B.C., cast bronze, 3", good+ **$55**

Ax. Bronze Age, Luristan, eastern Iran, socket, round poll decoration at top, 8", good+ **$550**

Ax. Copper Age, decorated shaft, good **$357**

Ax. Dated 1770, wood handle, 24 1/2" tall, edge 16", surface clean w/o pitting, good **$990**

Ax. Black Raven, double bitted, old handle, strong embossing, good **$82**

Ax. French doloire, touch marks, decoration, recessed panels, applied edge, handle has some age, good.... **$264**

Ax. French doloire, edge 12", replacement handle, good **$99**

Ax. French cooper's doloire, marked but not readable, edge 13", head 6", early handle, good........................ **$104**

Ax. French, early, 19", edge 7 1/2", pitted overall, handle not old, good **$115**

Ax. Hand type, bronze, animal on topside, jade inlaid, short handle one side, socket other, good **$412**

Ax head. Bronze, socket for wood handle, checked design w/ animals on topside, blade decorated jade, good **$467**

Ax head. Bronze, socket head, jade blade, highly decorated, 9", good **$605**

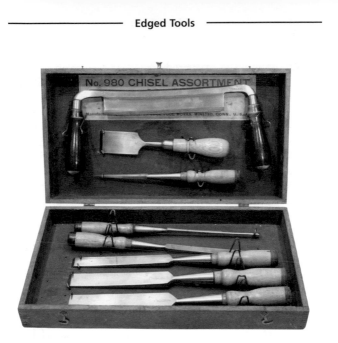

Chisels. Winsted Edge Tool Works No. 980, five No. 100 socket-firmer chisels, 1/4" to 1 1/4", No. 270 butt chisel, 1 1/2", No. 115 razor-blade drawing knife, combination reamer and awl, all are T.H. Witherby tools, wood box, good inside label, traces of outside label, fine, $495.

Basket maker's shaves. Buck Osier, brass, pair, one cuts width and has thumbscrew on end that controls width of cutters, other for thickness, hinged cover on thickness gauge reveals wing nut that adjusts thickness of cut, manufactured, fine **$137**

Block knife. French, T handle, edge 19", original staple, good+ **$82**

Blocking ax. Talabot, for squaring up heavy timbers, 20", little or no use, fine **$137**

Boarding ax. British, strapped head, original handle, leather case, good+ **$319**

Boarding ax. Strap, hatchet w/ curved spike, turned-grip handle, good **$165**

Bolt cutter. Possibly I. Penny (weak stamp), 18th century, turning rosewood handle advances edge to cut bolt, good+ **$77**

Bowl adze. Early 19th century, old handle, good **$143**

Bowl adze. E. Contangin, original handle, edge 5", good+ **$209**

Bowl adze. French, edge 8 1/4", good **$225**

Bowl adze. French, handwrought, two dished-out areas on backside, old handle, 8", good+ **$176**

Bowl adze. French, touch marks similar to a smiley face surround four stars, applied edge 8", old handle, no pitting, good **$236**

Carpenter's ax. French, marked but not clear, 12 1/2",
edge 9 1/2", new handle, good **$165**

Carving chisels. Henry Taylor, set of three, Nos. 93, 95,
and 97, large sweeps, 1 1/2" wide, new, fine................**$93**

Carving chisels. Various makers, set of 16, six match
and may be original, fitted wood box, spring-loaded
holders secure each tool in place and protect its edge,
good **$275**

Carving tools. Herring Bros., 23 chisels, walnut handles,
various gouges, assorted sweeps, 1/8" to 3/4" wide, cloth
roll, fine **$495**

Carving tools. Marples and other makers, set of 34, cuts
to about 1/2" wide, many handles match and others
similar, several replacement ferrules, good+ **$522**

Carving tools. Set of eight, mostly sweeps, mahogany
handles, fine.. **$165**

Carving tools. Swiss, set of 16 sweeps, 1/4-No. 31 to
1-No. 7, shallow to sharp bends, nearly new, full canvas
roll, fine **$220**

Chisel. Copper Age, about 4", edge 7/8", handle socket,
some edge chips, good **$99**

Chisel or scraper. Iron Age, about 3 3/8", edge 2 3/8",
handle socket, good..**$55**

Chisels. Buck Brothers, set of 12, graduated, 1/8" to 2",
all but two have original matching Buck apple-wood
handles, good+ **$577**

Chisels. Winsted Edge Tool Works No. 980, five No. 100 socket-firmer chisels, 1/4" to 1 1/4", No. 270 butt chisel, 1 1/2", No. 115 razor-blade drawing knife, combination reamer and awl, all are T.H. Witherby tools, wood box, good inside label, traces of outside label, fine **$495**

Chisels. Buck Brothers, set of 15, various sizes and types, new, original box for No. 30 handled firmer chisels, fine **$385**

Chisels. C.E. Jennings & Co., set of six, butt type, matching handles, fitted box, good+ **$220**

Chisels. I. Sorby, paring gouges, set of eight, extra long, boxwood handles, plus three boxwood-handled paring chisels, good+ **$225**

Chisels. Stanley No. 720, set of seven, long socket, 1/4" to 1" plus a 2", good+ **$440**

Chisels. Stanley No. 720, socket, matched set of seven, additional two w/ slightly different handles, sizes 1/4" to 2", good and better.. **$467**

Chisels. Stanley No. 750, socket, matched set of 10, additional three, sizes 1/4" to 2", good+ and better **$632**

Chisels. Stanley Four Square, set of six, wood handles w/ four red squares, similar to No. 750 chisels, canvas roll possibly original Stanley issue, good.................... **$1,650**

Chisels. Swan, socket firmers, set of six, one w/ different trademark, original oak box, label 75%, fine **$385**

Chisels. William P. Walter's Sons Hardware and Tools, Philadelphia, set of 12 Addis carving chisels, not all handles match, original wood box, paper label in lid, good+ **$148**

Clapboard slick. J. Dresser, early, edge 4", old handle, good+ **$82**

Cold chisel. Stanley No. 15B, beryllium, fine **$55**

Combination adze. Straight and bowl, old handle, good **$198**

Combination hand adze. Cooper's tool, early, handwrought, flat and hollow faces, applied edges, replacement handle, good+ **$104**

Cooper's ax. Decoration covers both sides, head 6 1/2", edge 6", replacement handle, good **$137**

Cooper's side ax. Bryan, Rochester, edge 8 1/2", old handle, good **$60**

Crooked knife. Carved handle, brass wire wrap, good+ **$82**

Crooked knife. Carved thumb rest, old green paint, copper wire wrapping on blade, good+ **$137**

Crooked knife. PIB, 1789, carved, taillike piece on bottom of handle, early body, later blade and copper ferrule, good **$198**

Drawshave. Stanley, fine **$825**

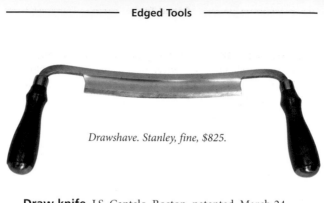

Drawshave. Stanley, fine, $825.

Draw knife. J.S. Cantelo, Boston, patented, March 24, 1891, handles fold inward to protect blade and rotate to adjust angle, 10", good **$110**

Edged tool. Japanese, bamboo handle, six iron rings, edge 7 1/2", good+ **$38**

Felling ax. Edge 10", head 13", old handle, good+ ... **$132**

Felling ax. French, faint marks on double touch, head 15", old handle, good..**$82**

Froe. Curved, old handle, chip on edge, good **$88**

Froe. Firkin, curved, old handle, good+ **$88**

Goose-wing ax. Pennsylvania, ogee cutout at top edge of blade, typical of P. Hiss, 9", edge 14 1/2", old handle, good+..**$302**

Goose-wing ax. Continental, left hand, two F-like touch marks, head 6 1/2", edge 12", old handle, some worm, good+... **$165**

Goose-wing ax. Continental, punch decoration, touch marks, applied poll and edge, head 9 3/4", edge 14", old handle, some worm, good **$220**

Goose-wing ax. Continental, touch mark, round back, turned-up nose, head 6 1/2", edge 15", old replacement handle, good **$176**

Goose-wing ax. Decorated, small eye, 8 1/2", applied edge 18", handle has some age, good **$440**

Goose-wing ax. Decorated, touch marks, small eye, 9", applied edge 14", handle not old, good..................... **$220**

Goose-wing ax. Early, large eye, some punch decoration, 7", applied edge 16", old handle, good **$165**

Goose-wing ax. Pennsylvania, left hand, 8", applied edge 14", old handle, some pitting, good **$275**

Goose-wing ax. Slipper type, heavy punch decoration on both sides nearly covers tool, head 9", edge 20", old handle, good+... **$165**

Goose-wing ax. Staller Wien, punch decorated on blade tail, head 10", applied edge 12", old handle, good... **$165**

Hand adze. Connecticut, edge 4 1/4", handle carved from burl limb and ends w/ modified deer's foot, good **$165**

Hand adze. Connecticut, No. 2, maker mark not readable, carved handle w/ handgrip and rest, good **$126**

Goose-wing ax. Pennsylvania, ogee cutout at top edge of blade, typical of P. Hiss, 9", edge 14 1/2", old handle, good+, $302.

Hand adze. Possibly for making large hollowed-out items such as dugout boats, old handle, edge 2" and nearly flat, good **$99**

Hand rail shaves. T. Tileston, Boston, matched left and right pair, marked, brass wear plates, good.............. **$220**

Hay knife. Swacick patent, Sept. 5, 1899, removable blade, original green finish, handle cracked, good+
....**$22**

Hewing ax. "Best Axe Made", paper label shows cooper working on a barrel, label 80%, old handle, good+
....**$137**

Ice shave. Plane type, cast iron, upright, four legs, cutter goes only part way across bed, wood base, couple of checks, some worm, good..**$44**

Mast ax. Possibly 18th century, applied poll and edge, faint touch mark, head 10 1/2", edge 7 1/2", old handle, good **$27**

Meat and food chopper. Double blade, rocker type, wood handles, good+ **$60**

Miner's track ax. Applied edge, wide flat pole for setting spikes, old handle, crack at head welds, good **$27**

Mitre trimmer. Lyon, two adjustable fences cut right or left mitres from 45 to 90 degrees, handle engages gear-action movement, good+ **$126**

Molding drawshave. Triple cuts, possibly for clock making, good..**$55**

Mortise ax. M. Beatty & Son, Chester, weak cow mark, old handle, good+ **$71**

Mortise chisels. Assembled set of seven, 3/16" to 7/16", good+..**$137**

Paring chisels. William Butcher, set of five, 1" to 2", matching octagon handles, wide, flat, good+ **$247**

Paring chisels. Smith & Co., set of 10, 1/4" to 2", matched handles, good+...**$495**

Pick ax. Stanley No. 69B, patented, beryllium, green paint about 40%, probably original handle, good **$209**

*Presentation ax. Red Mann Axe, Bellefonte, Pa., J.
Fearon Mann patent, Sept. 21, 1875, highly polished,
red-painted background, paper label shows Native
American chief, walnut display case, early handwritten
label on back indicates this was first ax manufactured on
April 21, 1875, first day of a 10-year lease, fine, $1,540.*

Plane-maker's float. Early, eight-sided, wood handle, good+...$121

Quill-pen pointer. "Rogers Cutters to Her Majesty", ebony, brass, knife slides out of one end and point cutter on the other end, good+ $192

Rabbet shave. Stanley No. 71, Sweet Hart, gunmetal, original fence, light wear, fine.....................................$192

Race knife. T. Symonds, probably maple, point, fixed cutter, swing blade w/ one cutter, heavy wood handle, some file decoration, good+.......................................$198

Router shave. Amesbury, Mass., heavy brass casting, gull wing, open handles, good+...................................$22

Shipbuilder's ax. Early, head slopes forward as it drops from eye, 16", edge 12", handle not old, good
....$198

Side ax. Possibly 18th century, decoration covers face side, applied edge, round eye, old handle, good
....$55

Side ax. Goose wing, touch marked, old upswept handle, head 6", edge 10 1/2", edge sharpened, good+ $220

Side ax. Robert Sorby, weak mark, old handle, edge 9", good+...$88

Slick. A. Joiner, Garrettsville, Ohio, 33" long, 3 3/4" wide, blade clean, no rust, good...$247

Slick. T.H. Witherby, original handle, 4", blade clean, no rust, good $247

Socket ax. Dutch, head 9", edge 6", old handle, good **$44**

Socket ax. Dutch, marked but not readable, head 10", edge 6 1/2", old handle, good......................................**$60**

Spoke shave. Ohio Tool Co., Stanley Model Shop, chamfer, probably working model of tool made for Ohio Tool by Stanley, globe logo on blade, no name or number cast into body, japanning 99%, fine+.........**$132**

Hammers & Mallets

Hammers closely followed the evolution of edged tools such as the ax, and some examples had dual purposes, one end for hammering, the other for chopping. By the 18th century, hammers had developed into a multitude of specialized forms and were used by a wide variety of craftsmen, not just woodworkers.

The most familiar type today is the claw hammer with the forked claw opposite the flat hammer face. The ball peen hammer featured a rounded knob opposite the hammering face. Although most old hammers had iron heads and later, steel heads, there are types that were all-wood for doing lighter work. As with most tools, mass-production did not get under way until the 19th century, and cast steel hammers only became widely available and affordable after the Civil War.

Ball-peen hammer. Stanley No. 4B, beryllium, original handle, good **$44**
Barrister hammer. Brass, rosewood handle, plating about 90% and dull, good..**$60**
Bill poster's hammer. A.R. Robertson, patented, Nov. 2, 1888, long two-piece handle for hanging posters high,

poster and holding clips, screw handle joint, good+
....**$99**

Bill poster's hammer. A.R. Robertson, Boston, two
sections, clips and holders complete, original finish on
handle about 95%, dull plating, fine **$137**

Bill poster's hammer. A.R. Robertson, Boston, three
sections, poster and nail holders, good+..................**$440**

Carpenter's mallet. E.W. Carpenter, Lancaster, possibly
rosewood, fine...**$50**

*Hammer. Possibly 17th century,
decorated, 11" long, good, $522.*

Claw hammer. "JP", miniature, handwrought, head just over 2", old handle, good+...**$60**

Hammer. 18th century, possibly earlier, ring design, turned wood handle possibly original, one claw broken, good, $302.

Hammer. Keen Kutter No. F4723, logo on head and handle, red and silver decal, 16 oz., fine+, $137.

File maker's hammer. 5", old handle, good..............**$99**

Hammer. Keen Kutter No. F4723, logo on head and handle, red and silver decal, 16 oz., fine+ **$137**

Hammer. 18th century, possibly earlier, ring design, turned wood handle possibly original, one claw broken, good **$302**

Hammer. Possibly 17th century, decorated, 11" long, good **$522**

Hammer. Soloman Anderson patent, perfect loop and arch, replacement handle, good+ **$770**

Hammer. Blake patent, Oct. 2, 1894, Cornish, Maine, combination nail puller and hammer, original handle, minor chips on jaws, good+ **$247**

Hammer. Double Claw Hammer Co., 1902 patent-date mark hard to read, old handle, good **$165**

Presentation mallet. Inlaid w/ ivory and at least five woods, L surrounded by two wood inlaid rings engraved on ivory plate, carved at joint between handle and head, fine, $687.

Presentation mallet. Inlaid w/ ivory and at least five woods, geometric designs around handle and head, L surrounded by two wood inlaid rings engraved on ivory plate, carved at joint between handle and head, fine
....**$687**

Hammer. Double Claw Hammer Co., 1902 patent-date mark strong, much finish bright, possibly replacement handle, couple of chips, good+ **$170**

Hammer. Stanley No. 1, Sweet Hart, handle decal perfect, finish 100%, fine **$495**

Hammer. Early, iron, decorative casting, good **$110**

Hammer. O. Fisher, early, sleeve to receive handle, one broken claw, good...**$22**

Hammer. Stanley No. 14NM, Sweet Hart, nickel-plated, mahogany handle, plating 97%, face may never have been struck, price on end of handle ($2.10), fine, $632.

Hammer. Stanley No. 14NM, Sweet Hart, nickel-plated, mahogany handle, plating 97%, face may never have been struck, price on end of handle ($2.10), fine ... **$632**

Hammer. Flat brass head, possibly horse-collar mallet, heavy, good **$176**

Hammer. John Habblewaite, patented, stepped back claw can be used as wrench, one claw comes to a point possibly for removing staples, old handle, good **$88**

Hammer. Peters patent, lasting, spring-loaded work ejector, old handle, some pitting, good........................**$77**

Hammer. G. Selsor, patented, March 19, 1867, faint mark, combination pane and claw, old handle, good **$55**

Hammer. Stanley, beryllium, finishes 90%, probably unused, good+..**$357**

Hammer. Unicast, double claw, patented, original handle marked "BB No. 8514", good+ **$77**

Log driver's rafting hammer. Heavy iron ring at base for hammer, point in end for pushing or sticking into a log, nearly new, traces of paper label, fine **$198**

Mallet. Carved, nude w/ bow on one side, nude standing at stair on other, fine **$396**

Presentation mallet. Ivory handle, ebony head, silver inlaid button engraved "AC", 7", fine........................**$550**

Rubber mallet. Stanley-Atha No. 697, early 1930s, new, original handle, decal 99%...**$187**

Mallet. Carved, nude w/ bow on one side, nude standing at stair on other, fine, $396.

*Presentation mallet. Ivory handle, ebony head,
silver inlaid button engraved "AC", 7", fine, $550.*

Saw maker's hammer. Early, old handle, good........**$88**
Stone dressing hammer. Brass-reinforced head, good+
.... **$160**

Levels & Inclinometers

Most people familiar with levels today may not realize that the earlier type didn't feature a "bubble" in a tube to operate. As far back as ancient Egypt, builders used a wooden A-shaped frame that suspended a weight on a cord from the top of the "A." When placed on a level surface, the weight hung perfectly perpendicular to the frame. This general style of level was used into the 17th century, and early American carpenters often made an L-square frame that suspended a plumb bob that worked on the same principle as the A-frame type.

At the end of the 17th century, the "spirit" level (i.e.– with a bubble tube) first came on the scene, but did not come into widespread use for 200 years. Since the early 19th century, spirit levels have been made, using either a wood body or even an ornate cast-iron frame to enclose the bubble tube. It is these handcrafted and decorative levels that are of greatest interest to modern collectors. More common examples can sell for well under a hundred dollars, while the choicest models can bring several thousand.

Bench level. Davis Level & Tool Co., pedestal, 4", unmarked, plating 80%, japanning 85%, good........**$121**

Bench level. Davis Level & Tool Co., pedestal, 4", brass ends, plating 98%, japanning 93%, fine..................**$165**

Bench level. Davis Level & Tool Co. No. 38, 4 1/2", good **$66**

Bench level. Davis Level & Tool Co., pedestal, 6", unmarked, japanning worn, good............................**$165**

Bench level. Davis Level & Tool Co., pedestal, 6", unmarked, plating 45%, japanning 70%, good........**$137**

Bench level. Mahogany, two ivory plumb bobs inlaid in brass top plate, 12", good+..**$165**

Bit level and rule. Green patent, March 31, 1891, screw attaches to tool, level can be set 90 degrees left or right, brass finish, good+ **$88**

Bowling-alley level. Starrett ABC bowling-lane gauge No. 636, 48", new, original box, includes new Empire pit end gauge, fine **$440**

Combination inclinometer level. Valentine, dial marked "Made in Oldham", walnut, level vial, 9", good+, $385.

Corner level. Davis & Cook, japanning 90% and bright, fine, $935.

Combination rule & level. Southington C. Co., flat, level, two plumb vials, adjustable brass vial holders, rule polished steel, 24", good+ **$110**

Combination inclinometer level. Valentine, dial marked "Made in Oldham", walnut, level vial, 9", brass plate and sole, good+ **$385**

Corner level. Davis & Cook, japanning 90% and bright, fine **$935**

Dumpy level. W. & L.E. Gurley, Troy, N.Y., serial No. 431102, World War II era, marked "US", probably for military use, scope 17 1/2", original dark green finish 98%, original box, good+ **$132**

Gauge. Stanley Rule & Level, eagle trademark, Williams patent, May 26, 1857, rosewood head w/ steel wear plate, brass beam w/ screw-adjust mortise points, good+ **$247**

Hand level. W. & L.E. Gurley, sighting scope, internal level, black finish 90%, leather case, good+ **$38**

Inclinometer. Chamberlain patent, Jan. 1, 1867, date marked on blade, arms pivots as degrees are read directly from protractor mounted on level base, plumb and level bubbles, body painted blue, good+, $165.

Inclinometer. Butler-Taylor Co., Ravenna, Ohio, patent applied for, level vial can be set at any degree around graduated 360-degree dial, can be clipped onto square blade, picture box fully readable but some wear, fine, $440.

Inclinometer. Champion, Philadelphia,
R.I. Frambes patent, Sept. 2, 1884,
graduating plumb and level, pendulum-type dial
w/ graduated scale, slide locks pendulum in place,
bevel glass face, hang hole, 16", good, $1,760.

Inclinometer. W.S. Batchelder, Pittsburgh, Pa., Chamberlain patent, Jan. 1, 1867, arm pivots, degrees read from protractor mounted on level body, one vial dry, good **$181**

Inclinometer. H. Chapin No. 306, boxwood dial can be set to any degree of pitch, 28", much original finish, good+ **$55**

Inclinometer. Chamberlain patent, Jan. 1, 1867, date marked on blade, arms pivots as degrees are read directly from protractor mounted on level base, plumb and level bubbles, body painted blue, good+ **$165**

Inclinometer. Chapman Hunter, pitchometer, brass, pivoting arm holds vial that can be locked at desired pitch, faceplate covered w/ scales and tables, good+ **$181**

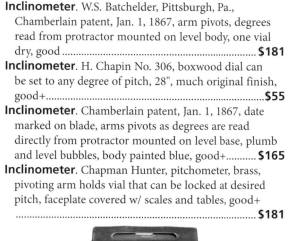

Inclinometer. Patrick Clifford patent, Nov. 26, 1867, cast iron, level vial attached to a semicircular graduated toothed dial, dial can be locked at various pitches w/ spring clip, 8", good+, $880.

Inclinometer. T. Cooke & Sons, Watkin Clinometer, gunmetal, brass, mahogany, adjustable dial, U tube, instructions on back, good+ **$27**

Inclinometer. L.L. Davis, 12", gold pinstriping 55%, japanning 92%, good+ **$220**

Inclinometer. L.L. Davis, mantel-clock type, gold pinstriping 80%, japanning 94%, fine **$385**

Inclinometer. Davis Level & Tool Co., square ends, 7", machining marks still on rails, japanning 90%, good+ **$247**

Inclinometer. Patrick Clifford patent, Nov. 26, 1867, cast iron, level vial attached to a semicircular graduated toothed dial, dial can be locked at various pitches w/ spring clip, 8", good+... **$880**

Inclinometer. Davis Level & Tool Co., 12", machining marks on rails 99%, japanning 96%, fine, $220.

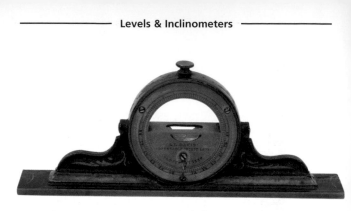

Inclinometer. L.L. Davis, mantel-clock type, even goes around base, gold pinstriping 97%, japanning 95% and bright, good+, $385.

Inclinometer. L.L. Davis, mantel-clock type, gold pinstriping 96%, japanning 97% and bright, fine, $440.

Inclinometer. Davis Level & Tool Co., offset inclinometer, pedestal level in center, 24", japanning 85%, good, $412.

(close up of middle)

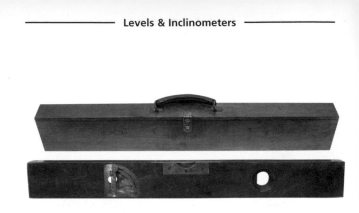

Inclinometer. Stanley No. 32, Frederick Traut patent, adjustable vial can be set to various degrees around quarter arch, owner's name stamped on top rail, much original finish, fitted wood box, both paper labels, outside label about 55%, good+, $357.

Inclinometer. Davis Level & Tool Co., 18", machining marks still on rails, japanning 95%, fine **$253**

Inclinometer. Davis Level & Tool Co., combination pedestal level and inclinometer, 24", no pointer, good **$275**

Inclinometer. Davis Level & Tool Co., 12", machining marks on rails 99%, japanning 96%, fine **$220**

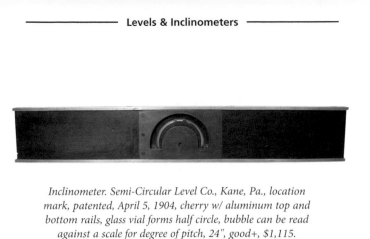

Inclinometer. Semi-Circular Level Co., Kane, Pa., location mark, patented, April 5, 1904, cherry w/ aluminum top and bottom rails, glass vial forms half circle, bubble can be read against a scale for degree of pitch, 24", good+, $1,115.

(close up of dial)

Inclinometer. W. Dennison, Hull, mahogany, heavy brass, large graduated protractor sets level arm, beam 52", good **$506**

Inclinometer. Eye-and-brow logo, boxwood, level vials on each leg, protractor gradations on joint, pitch tables, compass, gradations on sides, good+ **$550**

Inclinometer. Gibson Plumb & Level Manufacturing Co., Lahoma, Okla., patented, June 25, 1907, mahogany stock, plated nameplate on top, center glass dial w/ pendulum needle reads in degrees around a full circle, 26", clean, good+ **$247**

Inclinometer. Edward Helb, American combined level (levels, plumbs, grades, pitches, direction), dial crisp, wood clean w/ minor wear, good+ **$357**

Inclinometer. Melick, mantel-clock type, cast iron, dial in center, finish about 55%, good **$990**

Inclinometer. M.W.R. Co., Davis patent, 12", japanning 90%, good+ **$198**

Inclinometer. Stanley No. 036, combination, two-fold, 1-foot rule, folding scale and level, some original box, fine **$440**

Inclinometer. Stanley No. 32, Frederick Traut patent, adjustable vial can be set to various degrees around quarter arch, inside paper label about 60%, good+

.... **$605**

Inclinometer. Universal Level & Tool Co., Chicago, electrified version of Frank patent, Aug. 27, 1912, three mother-of-pearl buttons control lights at each porthole, compass inset into top, pop-up sights at each end, batteries go in caddy at one end, much finish and part of union label remain, good+, $1,760.

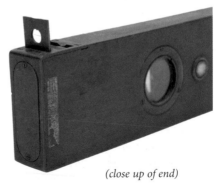

(close up of end)

*Inclinometer. F. Kraengel, Buffalo, N.Y., patented,
Aug. 17, 1880, marked "Pat. Apl'd For", later stamped
"Patent", mahogany, center porthole w/ two vials set at
90 degrees, vials rotate to set to any angle, silvered dial
graduated for direct reading, rule/caliper slides out of
one end, 16", much original finish, fine+, $3,740.*

Inclinometer. Stephens Co., patented, Jan. 18, 1858,
ivory, German-silver bound, level w/ adjustable blade,
couple of hairline shrinkage cracks, good **$385**

Inclinometer. Stephens & Co. No. 38, ivory white,
German-silver trimmings, metal bright and shiny, stress
crack in one leg, good+ **$2,200**

Inclinometer. F. Kraengel, Buffalo, N.Y., patented,
Aug. 17, 1880, marked "Pat. Apl'd For", later stamped
"Patent", mahogany, center porthole w/ two vials set at
90 degrees, vials rotate to set to any angle, silvered dial
graduated for direct reading, rule/caliper slides out of
one end, 16", much original finish, fine+ **$3,740**

Inclinometer. L.C. Stephens & Co., ebony, brass bound,
wood jet black, good+ **$4,400**

(close up of middle)

Inclinometer level. H. Chapin No. 306, boxwood dial indicator can be set for various degrees of pitch, 28", much original finish, good+, $220.

Inclinometer. Tower pocket level, patented, March 3, 1891, dial sets angle, can be clamped to rule, plating 99%, fine.. **$176**

Inclinometer. Troughton & Simms, London, brass bound, two-fold, 1 foot, opens to brass dial w/ pendulum weight, reads directly in degrees, pitch and temperature conversion tables on outside, good..... **$187**

Inclinometer level. Deck Gravity Level Co., patented, Dec. 15, 1896, large brass dial and faceplate, needle reads degree of pitch, 30", much original finish, good+, $467.

Inclinometer level. Deck Gravity Level Co., patented, Dec. 15, 1896, large brass dial and faceplate, needle reads degree of pitch, 30", much original finish, good+ **$467**

Level. Brass bound, rosewood, 6", fine **$176**

Level. E.W. Carpenter, Lancaster, marked, mahogany, adjustable, large brass plates hold vial, 26", good+ **$33**

Level. Crescent Manufacturing Co., ornate, open filigree, 6", japanning 85%, good+.. **$198**

Level. Davis & Cook, sometimes called a pretzel level, cast iron, pinwheel open-filigree work, 24", one lens cracked, good..**$330**

Level. Davis Level & Tool Co., 24", 2 13/16" high, japanning 90%, good+ **$242**

Level. Davis Level & Tool Co., pedestal, 4", unmarked, plating worn, japanning 90%, good **$88**

Level. Davis Level & Tool Co., pedestal, 6", refinished japanning 100%, good+ **$88**

Level. Davis Level & Tool Co., pedestal, 18", plating 98% and bright, japanning 98%, fine+ **$302**

Level. J.R. Grayston, from New York Level Depot, mark stamped into wood just above brass top plate, probably rosewood, 27", good **$60**

Level. C.E. Jennings & Co., open filigree, 12", japanning 95%, plating bright, fine...**$110**

Level. Davis Level & Tool Co., pocket, hexagon, 3", six sided, brass end caps, plating 95%, japanning 85%, good+, $110.

Level. Davis Level & Tool Co., pocket, hexagon, 3", six sided, brass end caps, plating 95%, japanning 85%, good+...**$110**

Level. Millers Falls Co. No. 10, brass bound, rosewood, 6 1/2", good+ **$330**

Level. Pedestal, Davis type, japanning 95%, plating 95%, 4", both screws original, good+ **$110**

Level. C.E. Richardson, Athol, Mass., cast iron, 6" in low profile, 7/8" tall, japanning 90%, good+.....................**$60**

Level. Springfield Level & Tool Co., cast iron, ornate, 18", plating 90%, japanning 97%, fine **$148**

Level. Stanley No. 13, W.T. Nicholson patent, May 1, 1860, 14", japanning 80%, plumb bulb dry, good+ **$105**

Level. Stanley No. 15, W.T. Nicholson patent, May 1, 1860, 24", japanning 65%, good.................................**$209**

Level. Stanley No. 17, new, original box worn, no label, fine **$192**

Level. Stanley No. 18, 30", light use, original box worn, fine **$105**

Level. Stanley No. 96, Sweet Hart, 30", most original finish, fine...**$82**

Level. Stanley No. 98, brass bound, 9", red I.D. paint on grip, good..**$231**

Level. Stanley No. 98, brass bound, rosewood, 9", good+ **$264**

Level. Fitchburg Level Co., Webb patent, Dec. 7, 1886, 12", one dry vial, japanning 85%, good+, $143.

Level. Stanley No. 98, brass bound, rosewood, 12", good+ **$286**

Level. Stanley No. 98, V logo, brass bound, rosewood, 18", few paints spots and dings, much original finish, good+... **$352**

Level. Stanley No. 98, brass bound, rosewood, 30", wood box, fine.. **$187**

Level. Stanley Four Square, original box, fine **$357**

Level. Stanley Rule & Level Co., brass bound, rosewood, 12", original finish 65%, good+ **$154**

Level. Stratton Brothers, brass bound, mahogany, double-plumb vials, 12", good.. **$110**

Level. Stratton Brothers, brass bound, rosewood, 6 1/2", "M.V.M." monogram (M.V. Mills) stamped on top in interlocking loops, brass lightly polished, fine **$247**

Level. Stratton Brothers No. 1, brass bound, rosewood, 30", good+.. **$160**

Level. Pedestal, bronze, raised, vial in center, open area below, 7", good+, $275.

Level. Stratton Brothers No. 10, brass bound, rosewood, 6 1/2", good...**$253**

Level. Stratton Brothers No. 10, brass bound, rosewood, 6 1/2", traces of original finish, fine **$357**

Level. Stratton Brothers No. 10, brass bound, rosewood, 10", owner's initials engraved on end, good+ **$192**

Level. Stratton Brothers No. 10, brass bound, rosewood, 12", good+...**$165**

Level. J. & G.H. Walker, New York, mahogany, 20", 1 7/8" tall, good...**$44**

Level and gauging device. Starrett, heavy machined iron frame, gauges distance between two points, possibly special-order item, 31", fitted wood case, fine **$165**

Leveling device. Horsfall, patented, for the "Alinment and Leveling of Shaft &c.", inclinometer sits atop shaft

Machinist's level. Stanley No. 45, early eagle trademark,
early carryover from the Hall & Knapp, sold iron w/
brass top plate, acorn finials, 8 1/2", fine, $605.

and determines pitch, original box, instructions, includes device for calculating pitch between two points, good **$203**

Line level. Rosewood, brass top plate and tips, ports for side and top view, hooks cast into top plate, good **$55**

Machinist's level. Stratton Brothers No. 10, 12", original box, fine.. **$495**

Machinist's level. Stanley No. 45, early eagle trademark, early carryover from the Hall & Knapp, sold iron w/ brass top plate, acorn finials, 8 1/2", fine **$605**

Machinist's bench level. Stanley, iron, brass top plate, 6", square 7/8", good+ **$165**

Mason's level. Stanley No. 35, c. 1915, 42", much original finish, good+.. **$198**

Miniature level. Stratton Bros., made by Paul Hamler, brass bound, rosewood, 4 5/8", fine **$220**

Pitch level.
Standard Tool Co.,
slide adjuster on one end
lowers to set desired pitch, V-groove
bottom, 6", japanning 98%, fine, $82.

Pitch level. Standard Tool Co., patented, May 11,
1897, adjustable stop at end of level sets desired pitch,
V-groove bottom, 12", japanning 92%, good+, $88.

Pitch level. J. Rabone & Sons, patent Nos. 1375 and 12278, hinged level vial spring loaded and adjusts w/ brass knob on one end, dial on end directly reads in 1/8 to the yard, japanning 90%, good+ **$66**

Pocket and square level. J. Sherman, New York, patented, July 19, 1855, label under vial, japanning 45%, good **$27**

Railroad track level. Veron Works, Stanley Sweet Hart level plate and vial adjustment, 62", traces of label on side, good **$132**

Sighting level. Stratton Brothers, brass bound, rosewood level, brass sighting tube on top, brass escutcheon for tripod on bottom, base level 10", good+, $220.

Sighting level. Ward & Bedworth, patented, May 29, 1877, based on O. Hanks level, vial holder flips up 90 degrees for plumb reading, japanning worn, good **$143**

Sighting level. Stratton Brothers, brass bound, rosewood level, brass sighting tube on top, brass escutcheon for tripod on bottom, base level 10", good+ **$220**

Spirit level. Possibly mahogany, decorative cutout body, 33", fine..**$110**

Spirit level. John Rabone No. 1098, 18", original box worn, fine...**$148**

Square level. Stanley No. 42, marked, brass, good+ **$60**

Torpedo level. Stanley Model Shop sample No. 5, rosewood, brass top plate, original model shop tag, fine **$71**

Machinery

This section includes a variety of large mechanical devices that were developed during the 19th century to perform specialized tasks. Most are floor-model styles, with the earliest powered by foot-operated treadles that later evolved into steam- or gas driven motor-operated types. Finally, by the early 20th century, electric motors provided steady and efficient operation.

Although not many collectors have room to display the larger machines, they do offer interesting insights into the Industrial Revolution of the 19th century.

Calculating machine. Fowler, magnum long-scale calculator, circular slide rule, watchlike mechanism w/ two knobs that rotate dial and move cursor, instruction booklet, leather case, fine **$82**
Dowel-cutting machine. Stanley No. 77, set of nine cutter heads (1/4", 5/16", 7/16", 9/16", 11/16") in original boxes, japanning 99%, fine **$1,155**
Dowel-cutting machine cutter heads. Stanley No. 77, sizes 1/4", 5/16", 3/8" (2), 1/2" (2), 5/8" (3), 3/4", most unused, original boxes, one w/ no label, fine
.... **$715**

Forge. Hand crank, iron, pan 18" in diameter, well used, good **$154**

Picture-frame mitre machine. Stanley No. 100, complete, rule, rule stop, saw, both thin stops for clamping screws, gold-painted handles, fine **$412**

Treadle former. W.F. & J. Barnes, tractor seat, pedals, one cutter, refinished, fine **$550**

Treadle lathe. Star, no chuck nut on drill, paint about 95%, pinstriping 80%, good+ **$308**

Treadle saw. Barnes No. 2, velocipede scroll, boring attachment (modern replacement), adjustable tractorlike seat, pinstriping strong and original, includes Barnes Catalogue No. 56, Feb. 1, 1901, catalog appears to be original, good+ **$1,210**

Treadle circular saw. W.F. & J. Barnes, combination circular and scroll saw, appears scroll-saw attachment was never installed, refinished at York school, fine **$550**

Treadle jig saw. Dirigo, manufactured by J.W. Penney & Sons, Mechanic Falls, Maine, wood body, fancy treadle, overhead rocker drives mechanism, red and black pinstriping on natural wood background, finish about 85%, fine **$3,630**

Treadle scroll saw. W.F. & J. Barnes No. 7, fine **$357**

Treadle former. W.F. & J. Barnes, tractor seat,
pedals, one cutter, refinished, fine, $550.

Treadle lathe. Star, no chuck nut on drill, paint about 95%, pinstriping 80%, good+, $308.

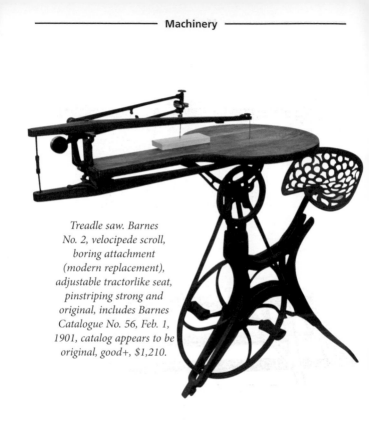

Treadle saw. Barnes No. 2, velocipede scroll, boring attachment (modern replacement), adjustable tractorlike seat, pinstriping strong and original, includes Barnes Catalogue No. 56, Feb. 1, 1901, catalog appears to be original, good+, $1,210.

*Treadle circular saw. W.F. & J. Barnes,
combination circular and scroll saw, appears
scroll-saw attachment was never installed,
refinished at York school, fine, $550.*

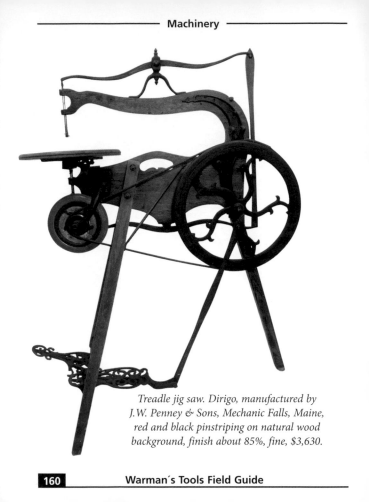

Treadle jig saw. Dirigo, manufactured by J.W. Penney & Sons, Mechanic Falls, Maine, red and black pinstriping on natural wood background, finish about 85%, fine, $3,630.

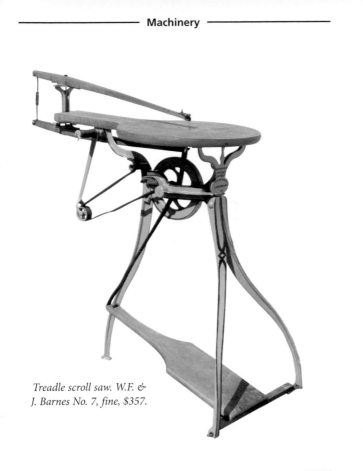

Treadle scroll saw. W.F. & J. Barnes No. 7, fine, $357.

Planes, Routers & Scrapers

In today's tool collecting market, older planes are probably the most popular collecting specialty. There are a wide variety of planes and related tools with blades used for trimming and shaping wood, and a wide selection is included here.

There is some debate among historians as to who first developed the woodworking plane, but it certainly dates to centuries before the Christian era. The plane first appeared in the Eastern Mediterranean region, and by Roman times, ironplated planes with wooden cores as well as cast-iron planes were being made.

In Colonial America, most woodworkers used English-made hardwood planes fitted with iron blades. It was in the first decades of the 19th century that a number of American plane makers started making and marketing their products, and by the 1840s and 1850s the first plane-making factories were built.

Some of these early English and American wooden planes were true works of art, being crafted with the finest materials, including rosewood, mahogany, ivory, and brass. Today, the choicest of these can sell for tens of thousands of dollars. Abundant wooden planes of more common hardwoods can be purchased for a fraction of those prices.

The end of the wooden plane era began in the 1870s when the Stanley Rule and Level Company began mass-producing ironbodied planes developed by Leonard Bailey. By 1900 the "Bailey" planes by Stanley had eclipsed all other types. Stanley remains a leading manufacturer of tools today, and some collectors specialize in tools made by this famous firm.

Beading plane. Union No. 44, handled, 1/4", no rust, good, $2,420.

Beading plane. Union No. 44, handled, 1/4", no rust, good **$2,420**

Belt maker's plane. Stanley No. 11, 1892 cutter, japanning 75%, good...**$77**

Bench plane. F.M. Bailey patent, April 16, 1889, No. 4 size, marked on iron, fine **$962**

Bench plane. L. Bailey patent, July 13, 1858, No. 1 size, marked on adjuster nut, vertical post, one of only two known, tote has couple of edge chips and hairline crack, solid back lever cap has two minor chips, japanning 90%, good+ **$28,600**

Bench plane. Bailey Tool Co., Defiance, No. 3 size, japanning 70%, good.. **$495**

Bench plane. L. Bailey, No. 4 size, patented, vertical post, Stanley Rule & Level iron, banjo lever cap, Bailey Boston adjuster nut, good+ **$3,630**

Bench plane. L. Bailey, No. 7 size, patented, vertical post, chips behind mouth, japanning worn, good **$1,595**

Bench plane. Birmingham Plane Manufacturing Co., slightly larger than a No. 1, smaller than a No. 2, Mosher patent, April 1, 1884, 6 1/16", iron 1 1/2", adjustable, marked cutter, japanning 70%, good **$1,760**

Bench plane. Birmingham Plane Manufacturing Co., No. 2 size, Mosher patent, April 1, 1884, adjustable, 7 1/4", iron 1 1/2", good+... **$1,760**

Bench plane. Birmingham Plane Manufacturing Co., adjustable, 14", iron 2", good...................................... **$275**

Bench plane. L. Bailey patent, July 13, 1858, No. 1 size, marked on adjuster nut, vertical post, one of only two known, tote has couple of edge chips and hairline crack, solid back lever cap has two minor chips, japanning 90%, good+, $28,600.

Bench plane. Sargent No. 407, oval trademark, japanning 96%, small edge sliver on tote, good+

.... **$165**

Bench plane. Stanley No. 1, c. 1880, japanning 93%, good+.. **$1,155**

Bench plane. Stanley No. 5, cork handles, B casting, fine, $38.

Bench plane. Stanley No. 1, c. 1930, traces of decal and base crack on tote, orange frog paint 90%, japanning 90%, good+ **$935**

Bench plane. Stanley No. 2, original box, fine......... **$825**

Bench plane. Stanley No. 2, second Sweet Hart, much original finish, japanning 99%, fine+........................ **$300**

Bench plane. Stanley No. 2, c. 1895, minor storage stain, original green picture box, full label, fine **$1,045**

Bench plane. Stanley No. 3, 1950s, new, original box, fine+.. **$115**

Bench plane. Stanley No. 3C, Sweet Hart, c. 1925, corrugated, japanning 98%, fine................................... **$77**

Bench plane. Stanley Bed Rock No. 602, c. 1915, corrugated, Bed Rock cap, japanning 90% good+, $1,870.

Bench plane. Stanley No. 4, Sweet Hart, original box, fine **$165**

Bench plane. Stanley No. 4C, Sweet Hart, corrugated, handle decal 100%, fine **$198**

Bench plane. Stanley No. 4C, V logo, corrugated, original box, good+ **$192**

Bench plane. Stanley No. 4 1/2H, Sweet Hart blade, japanning 85%, good **$990**

Bench plane. Stanley No. 5A, Sweet Hart, aluminum, full decal on tote, most original finish, fine+ **$225**

Bench plane. Stanley No. 5A, Sweet Hart, aluminum, new, original box w/ light wear and tear at corner, fine+ **$2,090**

Bench plane. F.M. Bailey patent, April 16, 1889, No. 4 size, marked on iron, fine, $962.

Bench plane. Stanley No. 5 1/2H, piece of edge off tote, japanning worn, good **$825**

Bench plane. Stanley No. 6, patented, type 3, frog mounted on vertical rib cast into bottom, minor edge roughness on tote, japanning 75%, good **$242**

Bench plane. Stanley No. 6, c. 1950, japanning 99%, fine **$50**

Bench plane. Stanley No. 2C, c. 1930, No. 2 size, corrugated, flake off top of tote, japanning 92%, good+, $412.

Bench plane. Stanley No. 7, Ready Edge cutter, tote decal about 90%, japanning 98%, fine **$137**

Bench plane. Stanley No. 7C, c. 1933, corrugated, new, George Worthington Co. store tag, Cleveland, original box worn but label good, fine **$330**

Bench plane. Stanley No. 8C, V logo, corrugated, japanning 99%, fine+ **$165**

Bench plane. Stanley No. 49, extra blade, original box, fine **$440**

Bench plane. Stanley No. 110, shoe buckle, type 2, straight sides, replacement knob, japanning 35%, good
.... **$236**

Bench plane. Stanley No. 2C, c. 1930, corrugated, original box marked C, fine+, $3,300.

Bench plane. Stanley Bed Rock No. 602, c. 1932, japanning 93%, good+ **$522**

Bench plane. Stanley Bed Rock 602C, type 4, corrugated, japanning 100% and possibly refinished, fine **$1,540**

Bench plane. Stanley Bed Rock No. 603, c. 1925, corrugated, japanning 90%, good+ **$275**

Bench plane. Stanley Bed Rock No. 604, new, original box, flat sides, paper inserts, corner torn out, red label mint, fine+ **$605**

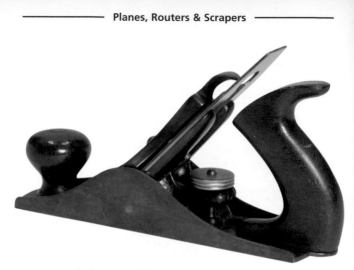

Bench plane. L. Bailey, No. 4 size, patented, vertical post, Stanley Rule & Level iron, banjo lever cap, Bailey Boston adjuster nut, good+, $3,630.

Bench plane. Stanley Bed Rock No. 604, type 3, B casting, japanning 95%, good+ **$165**
Bench plane. Stanley Bed Rock No. 604, type 5, corrugated, japanning 90%, good+ **$275**

Bench plane. Stanley Bed Rock No. 604 1/2, type 7, corrugated, japanning 95%, good+ **$308**

Bench plane. Stanley Bed Rock No. 605 1/4, type 7, japanning 95%, good+ **$302**

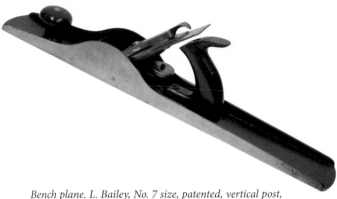

Bench plane. L. Bailey, No. 7 size, patented, vertical post, chips behind mouth, japanning worn, good, $1,595.

Bench plane.
L. Bailey, No. 5 size,
patented, vertical post, W.
Butcher iron, japanning 80%, good, $2,090.

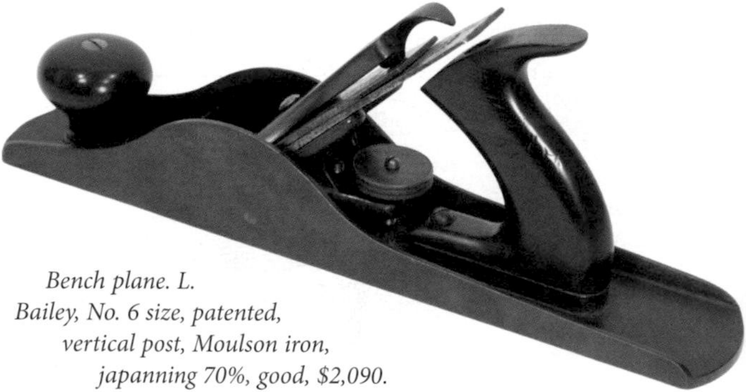

Bench plane. L.
Bailey, No. 6 size, patented,
vertical post, Moulson iron,
japanning 70%, good, $2,090.

Bench plane. L. Bailey, No. 8 size, patented, vertical post, Buck iron, solid cap, japanning worn, good, $3,960.

Bench plane. Birdsill Holly, smoother size, Baldwin Tool Co. iron, cutter 2 1/8" wide, elongated oval corrugations on sole, good+, $2,090.

Bench plane. Birmingham Plane Manufacturing Co., slightly larger than a No. 1, smaller than a No. 2, Mosher patent, April 1, 1884, 6 1/16", iron 1 1/2", adjustable, marked cutter, japanning 70%, good, $1,760.

Bench plane. Ohio No. 01, smoother, No. 1 size, marked cutter, much original finish, japanning 95%, fine, $2,860.

Bench plane. Birmingham Plane Manufacturing Co., No. 2 size, Mosher patent, April 1, 1884, adjustable, 7 1/4", iron 1 1/2", good+, $1,760.

Bench plane. Stanley Bed Rock No. 605 1/2, type 4, corrugated, proper cap, japanning 85%, good......... **$160**

Bench plane. Stanley Bed Rock No. 606, type 7, couple of paint spots on tail, japanning 90%, good............. **$132**

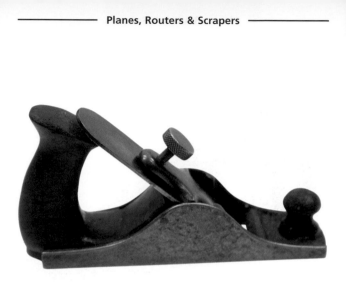

Bench plane. No. 0 1/2 size, Chapin-style screw cap, tote carved in bun style, infill fills all the area up to the frog, small button knob on front, inside of body and screw cap originally japanned in red, both handles have screws coming up from bottom, 5", iron 15/16", probably manufactured, good, $3,300.

*Bench plane. Gage Tool Co., Vineland, N.J.,
No. 4 size, metal body, round sides, short square knob,
probably prototype rather than Stanley made, traditional
Bailey profile, tote has old chip on edge, fine, $440.*

Bench plane. Stanley No. 2, second Sweet Hart, much original finish, japanning 99%, fine+, $300.

Bench plane. Stanley Bed Rock No. 608, type 4, japanning 95%, good+ **$154**

Bench plane. Stanley Bed Rock No. 608C, type 5, corrugated, japanning 80%, good............................. **$214**

Bench plane. Stanley, Sweet Hart, original box w/ some minor wear, label scuffed on one corner and faded, fine, $4,400.

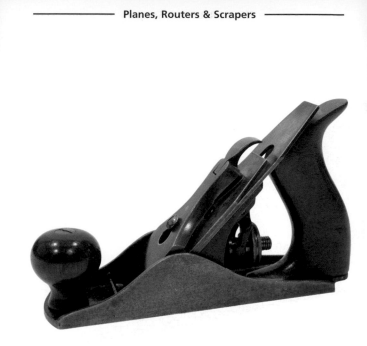

*Bench plane. Stanley No. 1, c. 1895,
japanning 95%, fine, $1,265.*

*Bench plane. Stanley No. 1, c. 1925,
japanning 98%, fine, $1,430.*

Bench plane. Stanley Gage No. 7, chip on tote, japanning 95%, fine **$165**

Bench jointer w/ fence. Stanley No. 6C plane, Sweet Hart, corrugated, japanning 75%, Stanley No. 386 jointer fence, complete, plating 96%, good+ **$137**

Bench plane. Stanley No. 2, c. 1895, minor storage stain, original green picture box, full label, fine, $1,045.

Bench rabbet plane. Stanley No. 10, pre-lateral, nick off edge of tote, japanning 90%, good **$176**

Bench rabbet plane. Stanley No. 10 1/2, S casting, adjustable mouth, much original finish, japanning 97%, fine **$286**

Bench rabbet plane. Stanley No. 10 1/2, Sweet Hart, much original finish, japanning 98%, fine **$247**

Block plane. Bailey Little Victor No. 50 1/2, adjustable, original red paint on inside about 45%, plating 40%, good, $357.

Bench rabbet plane. Bailey Victor, similar to No. 10 but no stop or fence, no holes for bolts in sides of plane, boss cast into body but nicker never installed, cutter nearly worn out, japanning 70%, good, $605.

Blind nailing plane. Stanley No. 96, marked on side, I. Sorby chisel, fine **$154**

Block plane. Bailey Little Victor No. 50 1/2, adjustable, original red paint on inside about 45%, plating 40%, good **$357**

Block plane. Birdsill Holly, patented, earliest shoe-buckle design, cast brass wedge to tighten lever cap, replacement knob, chip on receiver, 9", iron 1 13⁄16", scarcer than shorter types, good+, $880.

Block plane. L. Bailey Little Victor, non-adjustable, complete, japanning worn, good **$242**

Block plane. L. Bailey Victor No. 0, patented, non-adjustable, japanning worn, good.............................. **$297**

Block plane. G.P. Davidson, patented, April 1, 1902, cast-iron body, wood infill, name and patent-date mark on side in oval, good+, $302.

Block plane. L. Bailey Victor No. 0, patented, non-adjustable, japanning 90% and bright, fine.............. **$412**

Block plane. L. Bailey Victor No. 1, patented, adjustable, minor wear at mouth, japanning 50%, good **$247**

Block plane. Birdsill Holly, patented, earliest shoe-buckle design, cast brass wedge to tighten lever cap, replacement knob, chip on receiver, 9", iron 11 3/16", scarcer than shorter types, good+ **$880**

Block plane. G.P. Davidson, patented, April 1, 1902, cast-iron body, wood infill, name and patent-date mark on side in oval, good+.. **$302**

Block plane. Metallic Plane Co., Boston, patented, adjustable, shield decoration on cap, marked blade, 9", japanning 60%, good.. **$495**

Block plane. Ohio Tool Co., globe-cutter logo, tailed, rosewood knob, 7", good... **$297**

Block plane. Standard Tool Co., patented, brass lock cap wheel and adjuster screw, cutter marked, japanning 75%, good.. **$1,870**

Block plane. Stanley No. 9 1/2, type 2, pebbled cap, lever adjuster, japanning 85%, good **$126**

Block plane. Metallic Plane Co., Boston, patented, adjustable, shield decoration on cap, marked blade, 9", japanning 60%, good, $495.

Block plane. Stanley No. 9 3/4, tailed, japanning 85%, good+ **$275**

Block plane. Stanley No. 15, type 3, Bailey logo etched on side, logo 90% and fully readable, japanning 92%, fine **$1,980**

Block plane. Stanley No. 15 1/2, name stamp, earlier type w/o grip on sides, tailed, japanning 85% and bright, good+ **$374**

Block plane. Stanley No. 15 1/2, type 2, tailed, wood refinished, japanning 85% and bright, good+ **$286**

Block plane. Stanley No. 18, 1950s, original box worn, fine **$121**

Block plane. Standard Tool Co., patented, brass lock cap wheel and adjuster screw, cutter marked, japanning 75%, good, $1,870.

*Block plane. Bailey Tool Co., bottom corrugated w/
company name, non-adjustable, mouth has two corner
chips, replacement knob, japanning 80%, good, $962.*

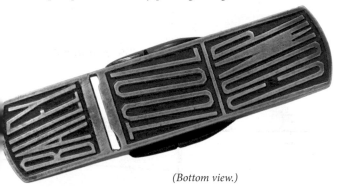

(Bottom view.)

Block plane. Stanley No. 18, original box worn, fine+ **$154**

Block plane. Stanley No. 18A, Sweet Hart, aluminum, ID blue paint on body under cap, plating 94%, good+ **$198**

Block plane. Stanley No. 18A, second Sweet Hart, aluminum, plating 75%, good+ **$176**

Block plane. Stanley No. 120 prototype, Stanley Model Shop No. 58, folded steel body Traut & Richards patent, Oct. 5, 1875, Liberty Bell adjustment Traut & Richards patent, April 18, 1876, lever cap redesigned Bailey patent, rosewood button, cap possibly early knuckle-cap design, unused, some dirt, fine, $742.

Block plane. Ohio Tool Co., tailed, cast-iron lever doubles as adjuster and lateral level, japanning 92%, good+, $1,100.

Block plane. Stanley No. 18S, c. 1930, original box worn, fine+.. **$550**

Block plane. Stanley No. 60, number mark, S casting, low angle, non-adjustable mouth, japanning 90%, good+ **$176**

Block plane. Stanley No. 60, type 1, tail marked, non-adjustable mouth, plating 90%, good+ **$60**

Block plane. Stanley No. 60, type 4, original box mint, fine..**$286**

Block plane. Stanley No. 61, marked "No. 61", low angle, non-adjustable mouth, japanning 90%, good+ **$132**

Block plane. Stanley No. 63, Sweet Hart, low angle, some storage stain, original box dirty w/ light wear, good+ **$687**

Block plane. Stanley No. 95, edge trimmer, original box worn, fine..**$198**

Block plane. Victor No. 12, patented, good blade, proper parts, japanning 55%, good, $467.

Block plane. Bailey Tool Co., Defiance, No. 4 size, adjustable, inside lever cam lock, japanning 60%, good, $1,100.

Block plane. Stanley No. 102, original green box, good+ **$165**

Block plane. Stanley No. 103, original orange box, early green label, fine **$170**

Block plane. Stanley No. 110, type 2, straight sides, shoe-buckle cap, japanning 65%, good **$495**

Block plane. Stanley No. 120 prototype, Stanley Model Shop No. 58, folded steel body Traut & Richards patent, Oct. 5, 1875, Liberty Bell adjustment Traut & Richards patent, April 18, 1876, lever cap redesigned Bailey patent, rosewood button, cap possibly early knuckle-cap design, unused, some dirt, fine **$742**

*Block plane. Henry Foss patented, Feb. 6, 1877, No. 2,
adjustable cutter and mouth, rosewood palm rest on
end of two-piece cap, japanning 95%, good, $4,180.*

Block plane. Stanley No. 201, c. 1900, nickel plating
80%, blade marked, good.. **$275**
Block plane. Stanley No. 220, 1960s, experimental
aluminum cap, maroon finish 100%, original box, fine+
.... **$192**

Block plane. Metallic Plane Co., Boston, patented, adjustable, six-pointed daisy decoration on cap, cutter marked "American Mfg. Co. Phila.", tiny chip on one side of mouth, japanning 90%, good+, $1,320.

Block plane. Stanley Bed Rock No. 602, type 6, second Sweet Hart, japanning 96%, fine............................... **$797**

Block plane. Stanley Bed Rock No. 603, type 6, japanning 90%, good+ **$231**

Block plane. Stanley Bed Rock No. 604 1/2, type 6, japanning 90%, good.. **$264**

Block plane. Victor No. 12, patented, good blade, proper parts, japanning 25%, good **$412**

Block plane. Victor No. 12, patented, good blade, proper parts, japanning 55%, good...................................... **$467**

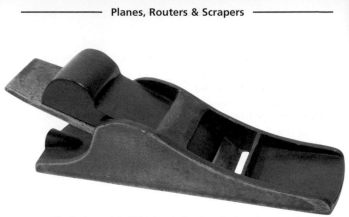

Block plane. A.L. Whiting & Co., bench plane logo marked on iron, 6", replacement rosewood wedge, good+, $88.

Block plane. Victor No. 12 1/4, patented, plating 25%, good **$825**

Block plane. A.L. Whiting & Co., bench plane logo marked on iron, 6", replacement rosewood wedge, good+...**$88**

Box scraper. Bailey patent, pull type, wood handle, cam-locking cutter holder locks w/ lever, 10 1/2", good
.... **$132**

Box scraper. L. Bailey, patented Oct. 3, 1876, pull type, wood handle, similar to Stanley No. 70, ink-stamp label on handle reads "L. Bailey & Co. Reversible Box Scraper. Hartford, Co.", good.. **$825**

Box scraper. Tatum, name cast into cap, cast iron, wood handle, good+... **$286**

Bull-nose plane. Stanley No. 101 1/2, japanning 50%, good+... **$275**

Bull-nose plane. Stanley No. 101 1/2, proper finger rest on nose, japanning 97% and bright, fine+ **$1,210**

Bull-nose rabbet plane. Stanley No. 11, probably made for British market, nearly full cutter, japanning 35%, good **$4,620**

Bull-nose rabbet plane. Stanley No. 11, probably made for British market, nearly full cutter, japanning 35%, good, $4,620.

Bull-nose rabbet plane. Stanley No. 90J, made in England, new, original box, fine+.............................. **$110**

Bull-nose rabbet plane. Stanley No. 90J, c. 1938, made in U.S., body and blade marked, japanning 95%, fine **$632**

Butcher block plane. Stanley No. 64, V logo, couple of paint splatters, japanning 97%, fine **$935**

Butcher block plane. Stanley No. 64, V logo, corrugated cutter, japanning 100%, fine+ **$2,860**

Cabinetmaker's block plane. Stanley No. 9, c. 1908, hot dog, minor pitting on dog and sole, japanning 80%, good **$687**

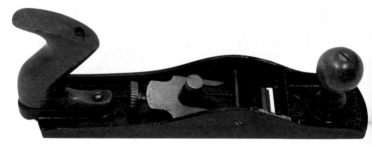

Butcher block plane. Stanley No. 64, V logo, couple of paint splatters, japanning 97%, fine, $935.

Bull-nose rabbet plane. Edward Preston & Sons, 7/8" of blade remains, japanning 80%, good+, $192.

Butcher block plane.
Stanley No. 64, V logo,
couple of paint splatters,
japanning 97%, fine, $935.

*Butcher block plane iron. Stanley No. 64, slotted,
probably unused, fine, $880.*

*Butcher block plane. Stanley No. 64, V logo, crack along one
edge of top of tote, japanning 92%, good, $715.*

Butcher block plane. Stanley No. 64, V logo, corrugated cutter, japanning 100%, fine+, $2,860.

Cabinetmaker's block plane. Stanley No. 9, type 2, horizontal adjuster projects out back of body, body perfect, polished surfaces, nicked corners on cap, good+ **$990**

Cabinetmaker's rabbet plane. Stanley No. 90A, cutter marked and about 1" usable, plating 85% and bright, good+... **$1,705**

Cabinetmaker's rabbet plane. Stanley No. 94, Sweet Hart, marked on nose, plating 97%, fine.................. **$495**

Carriage maker's bench rabbet plane. Stanley No. 10, pre-lateral, later blade, repainted, tight crack in knob, good **$154**

Cabinetmaker's block plane. Stanley No. 9, type 2, horizontal adjuster projects out back of body, body perfect, polished surfaces, nicked corners on cap, good+, $990.

Carriage maker's bench rabbet plane. Stanley No. 10 1/4, japanning 85%, good+ **$374**

Carriage maker's bench rabbet plane. Stanley No. 10 1/4, c. 1930, tilting handles, most original finish, japanning nearly 100%, fine.................................... **$1,320**

Carriage maker's bench rabbet plane. Stanley No. 10 1/2, type 1A, adjustable mouth, first lateral level w/ squared-off end, no roller, japanning 50%, good...... **$286**

Cabinetmaker's block plane. Stanley No. 9, type 2, horizontal adjuster, crack in adjustable mouth screw in nose, some chipping behind mouth, solid back lever cap w/ minor edge chip, 1892-patent replacement blade, good, $797.

Cabinetmaker's block plane. Stanley No. 9, c. 1895, finish about 85%, good, $907.

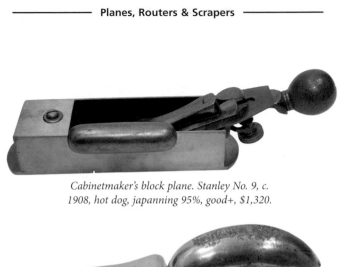

Cabinetmaker's block plane. Stanley No. 9, c. 1908, hot dog, japanning 95%, good+, $1,320.

Cabinetmaker's rabbet plane. Stanley No. 90A, cutter marked and about 1" usable, plating 90% and bright, good+, $2,530.

Carriage maker's circular plow plane. Thomas Falconer, rosewood, brass, awarded silver medal from Royal Society of Arts in 1846 for flexible steel fence and hollow-faced iron that combined as a nicker and cutting iron, fine...**$31,900**

Carriage maker's plow plane. Beech and oak, tailed, copper skate and wear plates, fiddlehead handle, good+ **$357**

Carriage maker's plow plane. French style, chestnut handle, steel body, brass fence controlled by threaded rod adjustment, wood turned up at nose for thumb rest, fine **$440**

Carriage maker's plow plane. C. Haberecht, Schwerin, "L/M N. 27 1875", maker name on brass adjustment knob, brass frame, quarter-sawn maple body, brass fence, screw adjustment, curved iron and wedge, brass wing nut adjusts steel stop, fine **$1,430**

Carriage maker's plow plane. Mahogany, copper wear plates, fiddlehead tail, adjustable fence, good..........**$176**

Carriage maker's rabbet plane. Stanley No. 10 1/2, early, S casting, adjustable mouth, 5/8" of blade remains, japanning 80%, good..**$209**

Carriage maker's router. Adjustable fence w/ interchangeable face plates, wedge cutter and nicker, fence slides in a tee slot, interchangeable faces held to sliding section w/ dovetail, good+..............................**$220**

Carriage maker's plow plane. S. Courcelles No. 110A, Paris, fruitwood, brass plate w/maker mark on side, screw arm, 6 1/2", good+, $165.

Carriage maker's bench rabbet plane. Stanley No. 10 1/4C, Sweet Hart, corrugated, japanning 95%, fine, $3,300.

Carriage maker's block plane. Stanley No. 9, hot dog, japanning 92%, fine, $3,740.

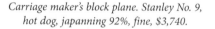

Carriage maker's fenced plow plane. French, beech, steel wedge and stop, brass fitting, screw-adjustable fence, good+, $495.

Carriage maker's plow plane. French, early, cast-brass fence, stop wing nut, wood wedge probably old replacement, some worm, good, $440.

Carriage maker's router. Amesbury, Mass., brass, inlay possibly cherry, 16", good+ **$275**

Carriage maker's router. Double gunmetal, fence slides for adjustment, good **$154**

Cased rabbet plane. Stanley No. 90, mouth tight, traces of original finish, plating 90%, fine **$165**

Chamfer plane. Mander & Dillin, Philadelphia, "Pat. Ap'd For", mouth slightly different from post-patent types, fine **$176**

Carriage maker's router. Adjustable fence w/ interchangeable face plates, wedge cutter and nicker, fence slides in a tee slot, good+, $220.

Chamfer plane. E. Preston, maker stamp, brass wear plate on nose, adjustable fence, fine............................**$99**

Chamfer plane. Stanley No. 72, bull nose, japanning 65%, good...**$253**

Chamfer plane. Stanley No. 72, Sweet Hart, bull nose, original box w/ edge wear, fine+ **$3,850**

Chamfer plane. Stanley No. 72 1/2, beading attachment w/ body, bull-nose attachment, japanning 95%, fine

....**$577**

Chisel plane. Stanley No. 97, Sweet Hart, no side reinforcement on body, edge clip on nose, japanning 85%, good...**$132**

Chisel plane. Stanley No. 97, Sweet Hart, japanning 95%, good+...**$352**

Chute board plane. Jones, "FL" owner mark in early paint decoration, adjustable mouth, screw cap, single iron cutter, no bosses on end for shooting frame, clip on handle and rail, good, $825.

Cigar-lighter spill plane. H.W. Yates, faint label lists directions and manufacturer, 9 7/8", good+, $181.

Circular plane. L. Bailey No. 13, first type manufactured by Bailey before March 28, 1871, patent, 1867 Bailey patent-date stamp on cutter and cap, Bailey 1858 and 1867 patent-date stamps on solid adjuster nut, banjo spring on lever cap, japanning 98%, fine, $1,870.

*Circular plane. Union No. 411, nearly new,
original box taped and worn, picture label
nearly full but w/clear tape over it, fine, $275.*

Chisel plane. Stanley No. 97, second Sweet Hart, chip on
nose, minor pitting on tail, japanning 93%, good+
.... **$275**

Chute board plane. Jones, "FL" owner mark in fancy
early paint decoration, adjustable mouth, screw cap,
single iron cutter, no bosses on end for shooting frame,
clip on edge of handle and rail, good........................ **$825**

Circular plane. L. Bailey Victor No. 20, later type, lever-locking cap, L. Bailey buttons on both ends, key-shaped sole adjuster, most milling marks visible on sole, plating bright and shiny, japanning 97%, fine+, $880.

Chute board plane. J. Mannebach, New York, beech, left and right skewed irons 4 7/8", handle on top, 34", good+ **$192**

Cigar-lighter spill plane. H.W. Yates, faint label lists directions and manufacturer, 9 7/8", good+ **$181**

Circular plane. L. Bailey No. 13, first type manufactured by Bailey before March 28, 1871, patent, 1867 Bailey patent-date stamp on cutter and cap, Bailey 1858 and

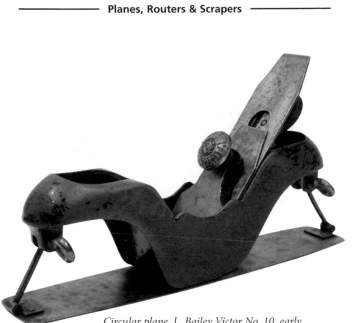

Circular plane. L. Bailey Victor No. 10, early cutter adjuster, japanning 60%, good, $192.

1867 patent-date stamps on solid adjuster nut, banjo spring on lever cap, japanning 98%, fine.............. **$1,870**
Circular plane. L. Bailey Victor No. 20, later type, lever-locking cap, L. Bailey buttons on both ends, key-shaped

Circular plane. George Evans patent, Jan. 28, 1862, type 1, shield cutouts for rabbet blade, brass screw cap marked w/ patent date, good+, $8,250.

sole adjuster, most milling marks visible on sole, plating bright and shiny, japanning 97%, fine+ **$880**

Circular plane. Este No. 113, made in Germany, finishes 98%, fine **$198**

Circular plane. Fulton No. 113, Stanley-made type 8a, floral decoration on adjustment knob, japanning 80%, good **$275**

Circular plane. Keen Kutter No. 115, "KK 115" mark on knob, KK logo on blade, plating 95%, japanning 90%, good+ **$418**

Circular plane. Kunz No. 113, 1950s, made in Germany, finishes 75%, good **$176**

*Circular plane. L. Bailey No. 20, early
type, key adjuster, original medallions,
lever lock cap, wheel adjuster,
complete, plating 70%, good+, $330.*

Circular plane. Sargent VBM No. 20, japanning 90%, good+ **$110**

Circular plane. Sargent & Co. No. 76, plating 95% but dull, japanning 90%, good+ **$137**

Circular plane. Stanley No. 20, c. 1908, plating 88%, good+ **$187**

Circular plane. Stanley No. 20, c. 1910, owner's name on side, japanning 85%, good **$110**

Circular plane. Stanley No. 20, c. 1912, original picture-label box, fine **$852**

Circular plane. Stanley No. 20 1/2, c. 1912, large block-letter logo on cap, japanning 95%, fine **$176**

Circular plane. Stanley No. 113, c. 1895, lever cap, japanning 96% and bright, fine................................ **$192**

Circular plane. Union No. 411, marked on tail handle, plating 85%, japanning 95%, good+ **$330**

Coach maker's plane. Geral, T rabbet, wood handle, good+... **$137**

Coach maker's plow plane. Adjustable fence, unmarked but probably American, tailed handle, good+ **$110**

Combination plane. L. Bailey Victor No. 14, patented, plating 80%, japanning 90%, good+ **$1,760**

Combination plane. L. Bundy patent, Nov. 15, 1870, Mooresforks, N.Y., match and plow, handle at each end,

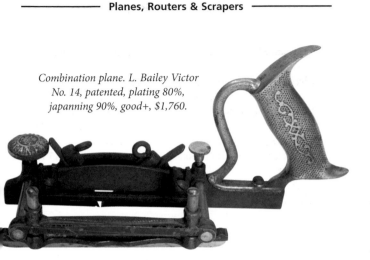

Combination plane. L. Bailey Victor No. 14, patented, plating 80%, japanning 90%, good+, $1,760.

center section is main body and supports other three
sections on two arms, fine **$19,800**

Combination plane. Lewin, universal, English version
of Stanley No. 45, aluminum body and fence, 17 cutters,
original box, good+ **$198**

Combination plane. Lewin, universal, English version
of Stanley No. 45, aluminum body and fence, 17 cutters,
original box, instructions, good+ **$187**

Combination plane. Ohio Tool Co. No. 099, similar to Stanley No. 45 but different panel design, three stops, two cutters, screws complete, no slitter, flake off top of tote, good+ **$247**

Combination plane. Preston, bull nose, fenced rabbet, chamfer, three fences (one rabbet, two chamfer), plating 96%, wood box w/ slide lid, fine **$1,210**

Combination plane. Record No. 311, rabbet, bull nose, chisel, interchangeable long and short noses, fine **$154**

Combination plane. Otis Smith, Fales patent, rosewood handles, one set of bottoms, japanning 90%, good+ **$357**

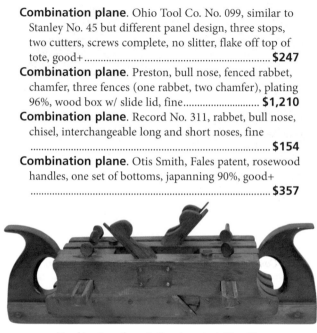

Combination plane. L. Bundy patent, Nov. 15, 1870, Mooresforks, N.Y., match and plow, handle at each end, center section is main body and supports other three sections on two arms, fine, $19,800.

Combination plane. Preston, bull nose, fenced rabbet, chamfer, three fences (one rabbet, two chamfer), plating 96%, wood box w/ slide lid, fine, $1,210.

Combination plane. Stanley No. 45, type 2, two stops, screws complete, 17 cutters in wood case, japanning 85%, good+ **$154**

Combination plane. L. Bailey Victor No. 14, patented, box at one fence arm broken, plating 50%, japanning 85%, good, $990.

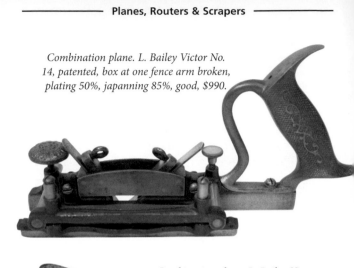

Combination plane. L. Bailey Victor No. 14, patented, plating 50%, japanning worn, good, $1,320.

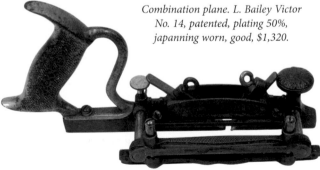

*Combination plow plane. Siegley, later style w/"Siegley"
on sliding section and "No. 2" cast into fence, 20 cutters
and short rods in canvas roll, plating 90%, fine, $330.*

Combination plane. Stanley No. 45, type 4, 13 cutters,
three stops, small nicks in tote tips, plating 90%, good+.
....**$88**

Combination plane. Stanley No. 45, 1950s, complete
except for screwdriver, probably unused, original box has
light wear, parts of label missing, instructions, fine
.... **$275**

Combination plane. Stanley No. 45, S casting, 18 cutters in wood case, plating 95%, original box, labels full and bright, good+ **$187**

Combination plane. Stanley No. 45, Sweet Hart, marked "Made in USA", screwdriver w/ about 80% of handle decal, original box w/ "Made in Canada" sticker, fine **$357**

Combination plane. Stanley No. 45, second Sweet Hart, complete except for screwdriver, original box worn, little use, needs cleaning, good+ **$247**

Combination plane. Stanley No. 47, slitter, two cutters, two stops, japanning 75%, good **$220**

Combination plane. Stanley No. 47, No. 46 type, first type w/ wedge slitters, no-hole fence, ground-off depth stop, japanning 85%, good+ **$605**

Combination plane. Stanley No. 50, 16 cutters in original wood case, complete, some minor storage spots, original metal box, paint 65%, good+ **$242**

Combination plane. Stanley No. 55, complete except for instructions, 55 cutters, screwdriver, original box worn, edges taped, fine **$1,045**

Combination plane. Stanley No. 55, Sweet Hart, 54 cutters, plating 95%, 1937 pocket catalog, original wood box, top label 80%, fine... **$1,100**

Combination plane. Stanley No. 143, last run marked No. 143 on side, most of wear on fence (copper

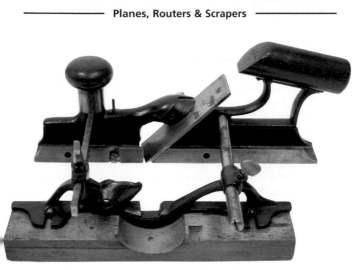

Combination plane. Otis Smith, Fales patent, rosewood handles, one set of bottoms, japanning 90%, good+, $357.

showing), much original finish on wood, plating 92%, nine cutters in wood case plus slitter, fine **$550**

Combination dado plane. Stanley No. 46, japanning 90%, two cutters, two stops, japanning 92%, good+ **$192**

Combination match plane. Stanley No. 146, smallest size in 140 series, plating 94%, good+ **$187**

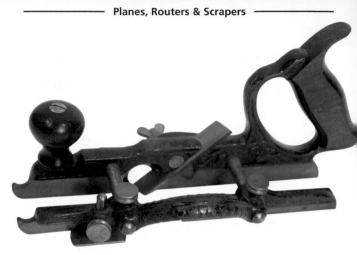

*Combination plane. Stanley No. 47, No. 46 type,
first type w/ wedge slitters, no-hole fence, ground-
off depth stop, japanning 85%, good+, $605.*

Combination match plane. Stanley No. 146, plating
97%, fine.. **$522**
Combination match plane. Stanley No. 147, second
Sweet Hart, plating 97%, fine **$165**
Combination plow plane. Siegley, 14 cutters, smooth
back, locking lever, solid handle, one stop, long rods,
polished surface, japanning 90%, good+................. **$440**

Compass plane. Oak, brass screw adjusts front section of sole, wood screw in bottom adjusts back section, 9 1/2", good+ **$247**

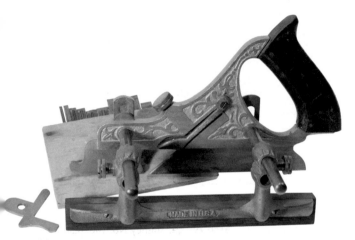

Combination plane. Stanley No. 143, last run marked No. 143 on side, most of wear on fence (copper showing), much original finish on wood, plating 92%, nine cutters in wood case plus slitter, fine, $550.

Combination plane. Jacob Siegley, patented, July 1, 1879, model presented to U.S. Patent Office w/original application, two wooden cutters, first Siegley production planes were modified versions of this plane, carved in pine w/ vine motif on sides, original patent office tag and ribbon, framed copies of original patent, fine, $19,250.

Cooper's combination croze and howel. Possibly rosewood or cocobolo, handwrought metal parts, good **$38**

Cooper's croze. L. & I.J. White, brass head, post type, strong stamp, fine **$154**

Cooper's jointer. Dated 1737 ("SP 1737"), carved w/ flowers along top edge and mouth, 50", replacement wedge, good..**$220**

Cooper's jointer. 9" wide, 50" long, iron 5" wide, good **$132**

Cooper's plane. D.R. Barton, sun plane, plane and blade marked, good+ **$110**

Core-box plane. Bayley, patented, Feb. 9, 1904, one cutter rotates as handle is pushed forward, pressure spring cracked, japanning 80%, good **$154**

Core-box plane. Bayley, patented, one cutter rotates as handle is pushed forward, japanning 95%, fine **$209**

Core-box plane. Bayley, patented, Feb. 9, 1904, one cutter rotates as handle is pushed forward, japanning 97%, fine..**$275**

Core-box plane. Gray Iron Casting Co., patented, Feb. 9, 1904, ratcheting mechanism advances arc of plane iron as tool is pushed forward, japanning 95%, fine **$330**

Core-box plane. Stanley No. 56, polished surface, japanning 97%, fine, $1,045.

Core-box plane. Stanley No. 56, polished surface, japanning 97%, fine **$1,045**

Core-box plane. Stanley No. 57, B casting, one set of extensions, proper turnbuckle and rods, plating 90%, good+.. **$154**

Corner-rounding plane. Stanley No. 14 4 1/4, patent applied for, japanning 94%, fine, $715.

Corner-rounding plane. Stanley No. 14 4 1/4, patent applied for, japanning 94%, fine, $715.

Crown-molding plane. J.B. Turner, Maine, yellow birch, offset tote, round top iron, flat chamfers, 4", fine, $467.

Corner-rounding plane. Stanley No. 14 4 1/4, patent applied for, japanning 94%, fine **$715**

Crown molder. A. Smith, Rehoboth, early, complex molding, round top iron 4 1/8" wide, top off tote, chip on nose of fence, good **$467**

Crown molder. Isaac Willey, ogee, bevel, lignum boxing, 2 1/2", good+ **$220**

Crown molder. I. Walton, double stamped by maker, yellow birch, round top wedge and iron, offset tote, 3 3/4" wide, 12" long, fine, $3,300.

Crown-molding plane. Late 18th century, round top iron 4 11/16", pull hole for stick or rope, 5 1/2" wide, top off tip of tote, good **$275**

Crown-molding plane. E.W. Carpenter, Lancaster, ogee, handled, applied fence, 6" wide, couple of checks in nose, fine **$935**

Crown molder. A. Smith, Rehoboth, early, complex molding, round top iron 4 1/8" wide, top off tote, chip on nose of fence, good, $467.

Crown-molding plane. I.D. Gilman, ovolo, offset tote, razee, 12 1/2" long, 2 3/8" wide, good+ **$198**

Crown-molding plane. Ohio Tool Co. No. 50, ogee, 4 7/8" wide, good+ **$192**

Crown-molding plane. I. Plank, probably eastern Pennsylvania, double marked in V shape, flat chamfers, handled, offset tote, good+ **$660**

Crown-molding planes. Matched pair make 7 1/2" crown, beech, fine **$1,650**

Crown molder. Apple wood, ogee, handwrought-steel diamond strike, 5 1/2" wide, good+, $550.

Crown molder. Jo. Fuller, yellow birch, pull stick, 5 3/4" wide, base crack on tote, good, $1,320.

*Crown molder. I. Sleeper, double
wedges and irons, strike button,
offset tote, 4" wide, good, $1,430.*

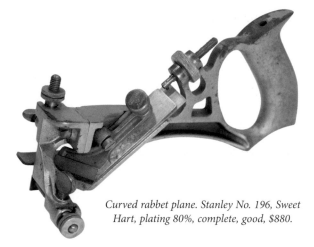

Curved rabbet plane. Stanley No. 196, Sweet Hart, plating 80%, complete, good, $880.

Curved rabbet plane. Stanley No. 196, Sweet Hart, plating 80%, complete, good **$880**

Dado plane. Stanley No. 39, 1", japanning 100%, original box badly damaged, fine+ **$137**

Dado plane. Stanley No. 39 1/2, 39 3/8 model, original box loose in one corner, fine+ **$220**

Dado plane. Stanley No. 39 5/8, new, original picture-label box, fine+ **$440**

Dado plane. Stanley No. 39 13/16, Sweet Hart, japanning 93%, rarest of the No. 39s, ground-out area by Stanley, good+ **$825**

Dado plane. Stanley No. 39 7/8, complete, japanning 90%, fine.. **$143**

Dado plane. Stanley No. 46, type 1, Girl Scout motif on low-rise fence, 12 cutters, japanning worn, tote has minor edge roughness, crossover depth stop, good **$1,430**

Dado plane. Stanley No. 47, type 1, four cutters, auxiliary fence on sliding section, top off tote, japanning 90%, good.. **$302**

Dado plane. Stanley No. 39 13/16, Sweet Hart, japanning 93%, rarest of the No. 39s, ground-out area by Stanley, good+, $825.

Dado plane. Stanley No. 238, Sweet Hart, special, 1/4", replacement small rod screw, japanning 85%, good **$132**

Dado plane. Stanley No. 239 1/8, Sweet Hart, original box w/ good label, one corner torn out, fine **$275**

Dado plane. Stanley Rule & Level Co., Rufus H. Dorn patent, July 16, 1872, manufactured in late 1872 only, first type w/ unsupported swing-out cutter, swing-out arm, japanning 95%, fine...................................... **$12,650**

Dado planes. Various makers, graduated set of six, wood, brass stops, skewed cutters, wedged knickers, good and better **$105**

Dado and filletster plane. Stanley No. 46, 12 cutters in wood case, original box worn, picture label 90%, fine **$3,300**

Door rabbet plane. Stanley No. 171, full set of cutters, japanning 97%, fine.. **$605**

Door router plane. Stanley No. 171, c. 1910, one cutter, japanning 90%, good+ **$242**

Dovetail plane. Stanley No. 444, four cutters, two spur blocks, plating 97%, original wood box well worn, good+.. **$880**

Dovetail plane. Stanley No. 444, four cutters in original wood case, no dovetail sample or screwdriver, plating 92%, original box, labels 85%, fine............................. **$880**

Dovetail plane. Stanley No. 444, four cutters in original box, both spur blocks, color instructions, plating 99%, original box, labels nearly full, fine, $1,870.

Dovetail plane. Stanley No. 444, four cutters in wood case, two spur blocks, instructions, screwdriver, sample block, plating 99%, original wood box, nearly complete inside label, outside label 85%, fine....................... **$1,100**

Duplex rabbet plane. Stanley No. 78A, Sweet Hart, aluminum, traces of decal on tote, good+................ **$467**

Duplex rabbet plane. Stanley No. 78A, aluminum, all proper parts, fine **$495**

Fiber-board beveling plane. Stanley No. 194, new, original box, fine+ **$33**

Fiber-board beveling plane. Stanley No. 195, new, original box torn in one corner, fine+ **$330**

Fiber-board plane. Stanley No. 193A, eight attachments, fitted case, japanning 95%, fine **$121**

Fiber-board plane. Stanley No. 193A, complete, instructions, original box well worn, fine **$126**

Fiber-board plane. Stanley No. 193A, complete, eight attachments, two rods, cutter box, new, original box worn, fine+ **$165**

Fiber-board plane. Stanley No. 1951, finishes nearly 100%, fine+ **$71**

Floor plane. Stanley No. 11 1/2, c. 1900, japanning 65%, good **$484**

Floor scraper. Stanley No. 43B, beryllium, brass handle, finishes 96%, fine **$192**

Furring plane. Stanley No. 340, replacement cutter and cap, chip along edge of tote, japanning retouched, good **$495**

Furring plane. Stanley No. 340, japanning 97%, fine **$1,760**

Furring plane. Stanley No. 340, patent date on cutter, japanning 100%, fine+ **$2,750**

Hand scraper. Stanley No. 283, complete, top-of-blade hand rest, japanning 90%, good+ **$187**

Furring plane. Stanley No. 340, japanning 97%, fine, $1,760.

*Furring plane. Stanley No. 340, type 1,
"Pat. Apl'd For" cutter, japanning
45%, good, $825.*

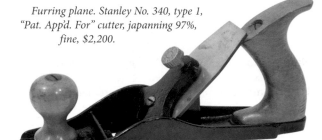

*Furring plane. Stanley No. 340, type 1,
"Pat. App'd. For" cutter, japanning 97%,
fine, $2,200.*

*Furring plane. Stanley No. 340, patent date
on cutter, japanning 100%, fine+, $2,750.*

Hand scraper. Stanley No. 283, complete, handle decal
45%, japanning 95%, fine **$231**
Hawk plane. A. Cumings, Boston, for striking a paint
line around the hull of a ship, steel wear plate, wood
stop, weak mark, good **$99**
Hollow and round planes. W. Greenslade, set of nine
pairs, No. 4 round recut from a No. 6, good+ **$275**

Hollow and round planes. W.H. Pond, New Haven, partial set of 12, all have J.E. Bassett & Co. paper label on side of nose, one wedge replaced, one broken, good+ **$302**

Hollow and round planes. Sandusky Tool Co. No. 92, set of nine pairs, sizes 1 to 9, many retain ink pricing marks on tails, fine **$770**

Horn plane. Dated 1768, carved mouth, lightly decorated sides, groove on one side probably for using plane in a pull stroke, good **$220**

Horn plane. Dated 1885, "INRI" carved into top, much chip carving, good+ **$60**

Infill plane. Robert Baker No. 142, 2005, instrument maker's mitre, brass, ebony infill, dovetailed steel sole, steel strike button, fine **$1,705**

Infill plane. Buck, mitre, rosewood wedge and infill, brass keeper, dovetailed, 8 1⁄2", cutter 2", good+ **$495**

Infill plane. Chariot, steel, ebony wedge, file decoration on wedge and nose, 3", good+ **$121**

Infill plane. Chariot, steel, mahogany wedge and nose infill, 6", heavy cutter 2", good **$105**

Infill plane. Craftsman made, jointer, walnut-laminated infill, gunmetal cap, 18", iron 2 1⁄2", fine **$385**

Infill plane. English, cast iron, brass cap, 12", snecked Ward iron 2 3⁄8", good **$605**

*Infill plane, Carter, London, modern, blade and
cap marked, gunmetal jointer, steel sole, dark
rosewood infill, dovetailed, Cupid's bow dovetails,
28 1/2" long, iron 2 1/2", two-made, fine, $5,500.*

Infill plane. Lancashire, pattern rabbet, mahogany tote,
gunmetal body and cap, skew iron, blade and sole at
90 degrees for shooting work, previously Ken Roberts
collection, fine..**$550**

Infill plane. A. Mathieson, shoulder, plane and iron
numbered 5, rosewood, dovetailed, 1 1/4" wide, nearly
full cutter, good+..**$165**

Infill plane. Milette, Quebec, 2004, shoulder, brass,
double screws for adjustment and blade holding, 11/16"
wide, fine..**$330**

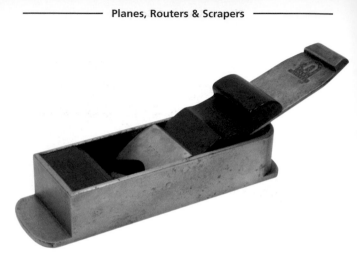

Infill plane. Buck, mitre, rosewood wedge and infill, brass keeper, dovetailed, 8 1/2", cutter 2", good+, $495.

Infill plane. Norris, rabbet, rosewood infill, dovetailed, 1" wide, cutter 20%, fitted wood case, good+ **$165**

Infill plane. Norris No. 1A, late type, adjustable jointer, ebonized stuffing, screws hold infill in place, gunmetal cap, 20 1/2", Marples iron 2 1/2", fine **$797**

Infill plane. Norris No. 5A, adjustable smoother, gunmetal cap, finish 85%, good+ **$522**

Infill plane. Craftsman made, jointer, walnut-laminated infill, gunmetal cap, 18", iron 2 1/2", fine, $385.

Infill plane. Norris No. 5A, adjustable smoother, ebonized stuffing, gunmetal cap, Norris iron, fine
.... **$577**

Infill plane. Norris No. 5A, adjustable smoother, hardwood stuffing, gunmetal cap, Norris iron, good+
.... **$412**

Infill plane. Norris No. 7, shoulder, rosewood, dovetailed, 1 1/2" wide, Norris cutter 90%, good.... **$385**

Infill plane. Norris, adjustable smoother, similar to No. 50A but w/ iron cap, walnut infill, parallel sides, Norris cutter 90%, good+.. **$385**

Infill plane. Norris 51A, adjustable smoother, rosewood infill, gunmetal cap, parallel sides, Norris cutter 60%, good **$396**

Infill plane. Preston, malleable shoulder, "Edw'd. Preston & Sons. B'Ham. Eng. Trade EP Mark" engraved on side, rosewood infill, 1 1/2" wide, cutter worn out, minor chips on top edge of wedge, good+.......................... **$302**

*Infill plane. English, cast iron, brass cap, 12",
snecked Ward iron 2 3⁄8", good, $605.*

Infill plane. Preston patent, bull-nose rabbet, right and left filletster, fence, stop, nearly full cutter, complete, japanning 85%, good.. **$374**

Infill plane. Preston patent, bull nose, side-fenced rabbet, chamfer, adjustable, plating 65%, good **$660**

Infill plane. Preston pattern No. 1347, bull-nose rabbet, cutter nearly full, japanning 90%, good+ **$99**

Infill plane. Milette, Quebec, 2004, shoulder, brass, double screws for adjustment and blade holding, 11/16" wide, fine, $330.

Infill plane. Preston No. 1351, shoulder rabbet, malleable iron, rosewood infill, 1" wide, 1/2" of cutter remains, good+ **$165**

Infill plane. Preston No. 1351, shoulder rabbet, malleable iron, rosewood infill, 1 1/4" wide, nearly full cutter, good+ **$165**

Infill plane. Preston No. 1363A, registered, bull-nose rabbet, 5/8" wide, good+ **$132**

Infill plane. Lancashire, pattern rabbet, mahogany tote, gunmetal body and cap, skew iron, blade and sole at 90 degrees for shooting work, previously Ken Roberts collection, fine, $550.

Infill plane. Preston No. 1368, shoulder, adjustable, 5/8" wide, about 3/4" of cutter remains, plating 85%, good **$330**

Infill plane. Preston No. 1368C, shoulder, adjustable, 1 1/4" wide, 1 1/4" of cutter remains, plating 85%, good **$264**

Infill plane. Preston, smoother, engraved "Edw'd. Preston & Sons. B'Ham. Eng. Trade EP Mark" on side, steel, dovetailed, rosewood infill, gunmetal cap, iron 2 1/4", good+.. **$990**

Infill plane. Preston & Son, bull nose, steel, rosewood wedge, 3 3/4", light pitting on sole, good+.................**$77**

Infill plane. Norris No. 5A, adjustable smoother, ebonized stuffing, gunmetal cap, Norris iron, fine, $577.

Infill plane. Record No. 042, rabbet 3/4", plating 99%, fine **$176**

Infill plane. Record No. 073, rabbet 1 1/4", plating 99%, fine **$198**

Infill plane. Spiers, Ayr, Scotland, smoother, marked in four places, rosewood overstuffing, dovetailed, gunmetal lever cap, 8" long, iron 2 1/4", good+ **$330**

Infill plane. Spiers, unmarked, combination bull nose and rabbet, dovetailed, rosewood wedges, 11/16" wide, couple of wedge chips, good+ **$220**

Infill plane. Preston, malleable shoulder, "Edw'd. Preston & Sons. B'Ham. Eng. Trade EP Mark" engraved on side, rosewood infill, 1 1/2" wide, cutter worn out, minor chips on top edge of wedge, good+, $302.

Infill plane. Spiers, Ayr, Scotland, jointer, rosewood, dovetailed, gunmetal cap, 24 1/2", Ibbotson iron 2 1/2", top of tote glued, tight crack in tail infill, good+ **$1,760**

Infill plane. Stewart Spiers, Ayr, Scotland, 27, smoother, marked in four places, gunmetal body, steel sole, rosewood infill, dovetailed, handled, some vine carving in wood, 7 1/2", iron 2", good **$880**

Infill plane. Spiers, Ayr, Scotland, jointer, rosewood, dovetailed, gunmetal cap, 24 1/2", Ibbotson iron 2 1/2", top of tote glued, tight crack in tail infill, good+, $1,760.

Infill plane. Stewart Spiers, Ayr, Scotland, 27, smoother, marked in four places, gunmetal body, steel sole, rosewood infill, dovetailed, handled, some vine carving in wood, 7 1/2", iron 2", good, $880.

Infill plane. Marked "W.A. Brown 1859" on side, possibly New York City, mitre, rosewood wedge and infill, wedge has brass center strip screwed into body, 10", Providence Tool Co. iron 1 7/8", small chip at top of wedge, good+, $385.

Instrument maker's planes. Graduated set of four, 1 1/8" to 1 7/8", brass, screw caps, fine **$302**

Jack plane. Birmingham Plane Co., patented, adjustable cutter, 14", marked iron 2", japanning about 50%, good **$275**

Jack plane. Stanley No. 27, J.A. Traut patent, Oct. 7, 1902, Stanley Model Shop No. 211, wood bottom, iron wear plate at mouth, narrow flat frog extends through body and forms flat sole for cutter, japanning 97%, fine **$1,045**

Jack plane. Stanley No. 62, c. 1908, low angle, much original finish, japanning 97%, fine, $330.

Jack plane. Stanley No. 27, J.A. Traut patent, Oct. 7, 1902, Stanley Model Shop No. 211, wood bottom, iron wear plate at mouth, narrow flat frog extends through body and forms flat sole for cutter, japanning 97%, fine, $1,045.

Jack plane. Stanley No. 62, first Sweet Hart, low angle, japanning 92%, ID line filed across top surface of tote, nick off nose of rail, good **$159**

Jack plane. Stanley No. 62, Sweet Hart, low angle, original box, fine+ **$4,950**

Jack plane. William Webb, Washington, D.C., "Patented Feb. 28, 185_.", wood, tight crack on tote, good **$105**

*Jack plane. Stanley No. 62, low
angle, japanning 97%, fine, $440.*

Jack plane. Sandusky No. 13SC, semisteel, new, original box near mint, fine, $3,080.

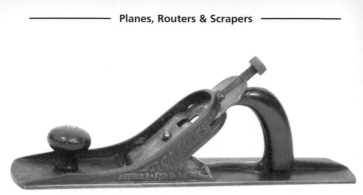

Jack plane. Challenge, patented, Sept. 11, 1883, body and handle cast as one unit, adjustable cutter (screw) passes through slot in body, 15", japanning 90%, good, $2,915.

Jack plane. Davis, screws on both sides, 15", tote reshaped at tip, casting flaw on one rail, good, $385.

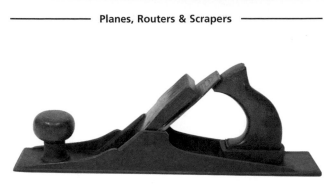

Jack plane. Knowles, patented, cast iron, open body, sockets for handles, wedge possibly old replacement, 15", good, $385.

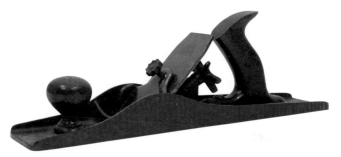

Jack plane. Rodier patent, cam adjusts pitch of frog, 14 1/2", japanning 70%, good+, $715.

Japanese smoothing plane. Rosewood, steel bar closes mouth, iron 3 7/8", fine.....................**$176**

Jenny plane. Ohio Tool Co. No. 037, japanning 90%, good+.....................**$110**

Jointer. Dated 1887, letter A carved in wedge, heavy chip carving, 25 1/2", good.....................**$154**

Jointer fence. Stanley No. 386, new, original box, fine+
.....................**$330**

Japanese smoothing plane. Rosewood, steel bar closes mouth, iron 3 7/8", fine, $176.

Jointer plane. E.W. Carpenter, Lancaster, patented, March 27, 1849, double wedges, 22 1/2", fine.......... **$242**
Jointer plane. Morris patent, Nov. 8, 1870, original iron, replacement wedge, chip off tail, japanning 20%, good **$990**

Jointer plane. Morris patent, Nov. 8, 1870, original iron, replacement wedge, chip off tail, japanning 20%, good, $990.

Jointer plane. Davis, patented, Moulson iron, tight crack in tote base, some roughness on side, wood polished, polished japanning 95%, fine, $715.

Jointer plane. "P.E.", 18th century, yellow birch, round-top wedge, offset tote, 25", good..................................**$77**

Liberty Bell plane. Stanley No. 104, tight crack on tote, japanning 85%, fine...**$126**

Liberty Bell plane. Stanley No. 105, early type, patent date on side, japanning 96%, fine...........................**$302**

Light plow plane. Stanley No. 50, Miller patent, 1872, date marked on fence oval, rosewood knob, acorn finials on rods and stop end, one of first Stanley plow planes, japanning 85%, good+ **$15,400**

Match plane. Stanley No. 48, original box worn and missing rear flap, fine...**$160**

*Jointer plane. Meriden
Malleable Iron Co., patented,
Feb. 10 and March 10, 1885,
japanning 95% and bright,
good+, $825.*

*Light plow plane. Stanley No. 54, marked in
several places w/ British broad arrow,
nine cutters, plating 99%, original
box, fine, $495.*

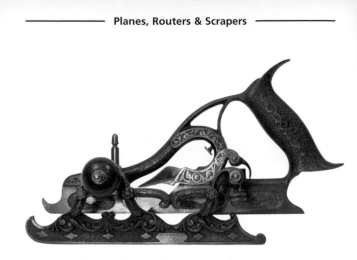

Light plow plane. Stanley No. 50, Miller patent, 1872, date marked on fence oval, rosewood knob, acorn finials on rods and stop end, one of first Stanley plow planes, japanning 85%, good+, $15,400.

Match plane. Stanley No. 49, decal on handle recess, Union plates, body ground out and painted black, plating 97%, fine **$275**

Miniature coffin smoother. Smith & Stewart, Springfield, Mass., beech, lignum stroke button, 4 1/2", good **$132**

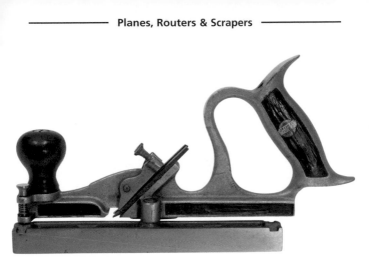

Match plane. Stanley No. 49, decal on handle recess, Union plates, body ground out and painted black, plating 97%, fine, $275.

Miniature plane. Compassed rabbet, brass, ivory wedge, 2 1/4" long, 1/2" wide, good..**$275**

Miniature plane. Brass, oval body, screw cap, compassed and radius sole, blade 5/8", good+ **$160**

Miniature plane. Chamfer, beech, adjustable stop set w/ screw on side, 3 1/4", good+ **$60**

Miniature plane. Coffin round, 4 1/2", fine...............**$77**

Miniature plane. Compassed rabbet, brass,
ivory wedge, 2 1/4" long, 1/2" wide, good, $275.

Miniature plane. Hatter's brim, Mickey Mouse ears,
brass, good+..**$71**
Miniature plane. Instrument maker's toothing, brass,
round design, cutter 3/4", good+..................................**$88**
Miniature plane. Leon Robbins, Crown Tools,
Bath, Maine, ivory sides, rosewood center, wedge a
contrasting light wood, 4", marked, fine **$82**

Miniature plane. Router, beech, good+ **$77**
Miniature plane. Solid brass coffin, cast brass wedge,
2 1/4", good...**$71**

*Miniature T rabbet plane. Birmingham Plane
Co., patented, 4", cutter 1 1⁄4", possibly salesman's
sample, two known, japanning 90%, good+, $6,600.*

Miniature plow plane. Marked w/ Ohio Tool Co. "Extra" stamp, probably made by Auburn Tool Co., 5/8 proportion, 6 1/2", probably salesman's sample, chip on one arm post, good+ **$2,640**

Miniature T rabbet plane. Birmingham Plane Co., patented, 4", cutter 1 1/4", possibly salesman's sample, two known, japanning 90%, good+ **$6,600**

Mitre plane. Roger patent, Sept. 19, 1882, double-skew irons, cast-iron table can be set for left and right mitres, faint lettering, green japanning 90%, good **$770**

Model maker's block planes. Stanley No. 100 1/2, two planes in remnants of original box for three, fine
.... **$275**

One-hand scraper. Stanley No. 273, orange paint 90%, good+ **$1,155**

Panel-raiser plane. R. & W.C. Biddle & Co., Philadelphia, adjustable fence and stop, skew iron, boxed, 5 1/2", good+ **$275**

Panel-raiser plane. J. Bracelin, Dayton, B mark, Ohio Tool Co. iron, fenced, stopped, wedge nicker, 4 1/2" wide, fine **$132**

Panel-raiser plane. E.W. Carpenter, Lancaster, patented, March 27, 1849, double wedges, fenced, stopped, 6" wide, fine **$2,420**

Panel-raiser plane. E. Clark, Middleboro, yellow birch, fenced, stopped, round top skew wedge, fine **$2,860**

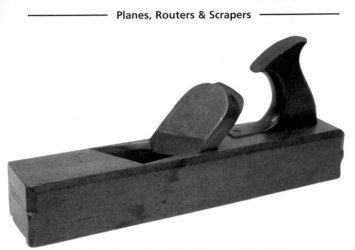

Panel-raiser plane. E. Clark, Middleboro, yellow birch, fenced, stopped, round top skew wedge, fine, $2,860.

Panel-raiser plane. M. Copeland & Co., for rounded panels, fenced, stopped, wedged knickers, skew cutter, fine **$396**

Panel-raiser plane. I. Custerd, yellow birch, newly applied fence, steel strike button, 12", skew iron, fixed stop, unusually narrow but deep tote, good+ **$192**

Panel-raiser plane. P. Dewit, probably American, 18th century, handled, adjustable fence, wooden stop, flat chamfer, top off tote, good **$352**

Panel-raiser plane. Thomas Grant, adjustable fence and stop, weak mark, good **$220**

Panel-raiser plane. E. Newell, Lanesboro, yellow birch, applied fence, round top wedge, Weldon iron, perfect tote, fine.. **$1,870**

Panel-raiser plane. G. Roseboom, Cincinnati, wood, adjustable fence and stop, good+............................... **$105**

Panel-raiser plane. G. Roseboom, Cincinnati, fenced, stopped, 4 1/4" wide, fine..**$88**

Panel-raiser plane. T.V. Shepard/R. Taft, yellow birch, fenced, stopped, gouge mark decoration along edge on front of throat, round top wedge, chip off sole at nose, good **$715**

Panel-raiser plane. N. Taber, adjustable fence, fixed stop, slightly curved panel, round top wedge, fine **$467**

Panel-raiser plane. H. Taylor, Cincinnati, adjustable fence and stop, good.. **$143**

Panel-raiser plane. J. Zimmerman, Kingston, Ohio, replacement fence, stopped, 4 1/4" wide, boxed, good **$88**

Pattern maker's plane. Sandusky Tool Co., aluminum body, irons, screw cap, wood soles, six cutters, complete, good+.. **$275**

Panel-raiser plane. I. Sleeper, early Yankee, fenced, stopped, skew cutter, Weldon iron, strike button 2 1/2" wide, good+, $1,540.

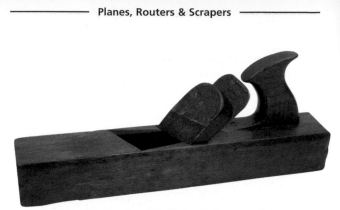

Panel-raiser plane. H. Wetherell, Norton, yellow birch, round top wedge, offset tote, flat chamfer, skew iron, 2 3/8" wide, 14 1/2" long, good+, $1,870.

Pattern maker's round plane. Harris, San Francisco, Calif., patented, wood soles have cast-iron side plate that dovetails into sides of body, one sole w/ plane, adjuster mechanism based on Chaplin patent, probably some original Chaplin parts, tail of plane marked "Pat. Appl'd. For", D.R. Barton cutter, good.............................. **$1,375**

Pattern maker's round plane. Simplex, two bodies, one wood body marked "4-6, 9-12, 16-20 radius. Wood Bottom made by S.R. S. Co. Handle & Knob & Cutter blank made by S.R. & L. Co. July 1915. E.A.S.", some parts probably Stanley made, eight cutters, all but one L. & I.J. White, marked plane has set of Stanley handles, fine **$330**

Pattern maker's round plane. Harris, San Francisco, Calif., patented, wood soles have cast-iron side plate that dovetails into sides of body, one sole w/ plane, adjuster mechanism based on Chaplin patent, probably some original Chaplin parts, tail of plane marked "Pat. Appl'd. For", D.R. Barton cutter, good, $1,375.

Pattern maker's round plane. Eight interchangeable bottoms and blades, brass body, wood case for blades, good+... **$170**

Pattern maker's round plane. Six interchangeable bottoms, coffin shape, six cutters in wood case w/ slide top, good **$71**

Pattern maker's round plane. Six interchangeable bottoms, brass sides w/ interlocking soles, six cutters in fitted wood case, good+..**$77**

Pattern maker's round plane. Stanley design but non-Stanley casting, aluminum body, four interchangeable gunmetal soles, one aluminum sole, bottoms stored in fitted wood case, fine... **$247**

Plane. Samuel Auxer, Lancaster, Pa., tongue, Carpenter patent split iron w/ improvements, two metal strips connect sections and make adjustment simpler, handle w/ adjustable fence, fine.. **$467**

Plane. American Manufacturing Co., Philadelphia, sold by American after Metallic Plane Co. closed, low-angle jack, cap engraved w/ diamond design, body w/ open-work sole, 14", cutter 1 3/4", good............................. **$550**

Plane. Barny & Smith Car Works, Dayton, Ohio, 1906, probably patented, Stanley Model Shop tag, wooden wedge w/ slot that slides over keeper, unused, fine
.... **$374**

Plane. American Manufacturing Co., Philadelphia, sold by American after Metallic Plane Co. closed, low-angle jack, cap engraved w/ diamond design, body w/ open-work sole, 14", cutter 1 3/4", good, $550.

Plane. Birdsill Holly, smoother, Dwights & French iron, cutter 2" wide, body smooth sole, 9", rosewood tote dovetailed to body, replacement knob, good+......... **$935**

Plane. Birmingham Plane Manufacturing Co. No. 3, Mosher patent, April 1, 1884, adjustable, 9", japanning 95% and bright, fine **$440**

Plane. Birmingham Plane Co., oval body, 4", japanning 65%, good.. **$220**

Plane. Barny & Smith Car Works, Dayton, Ohio, 1906, probably patented, Stanley Model Shop tag, wooden wedge w/ slot that slides over keeper, unused, fine, $374.

Plane. Birmingham Tool Co., No. 2 size, open cast-iron tote, adjustable, 7 3/8", iron 1 1/2", japanning 80%, good **$1,430**

Plane. Blandin patent, May 7, 1867, date marked on base adjuster wheel, No. 7 size, rocker-type adjustment w/ vertical adjuster, japanning 90%, good+ **$2,640**

Plane. Boston Metallic Plane Co., smoother, No. 4 size, patented, four-leaf-clover design on cap, Stanley blade, good+... **$1,210**

Plane. Birmingham Plane Manufacturing Co. No. 3, Mosher patent, April 1, 1884, adjustable, 9", japanning 95% and bright, fine, $440.

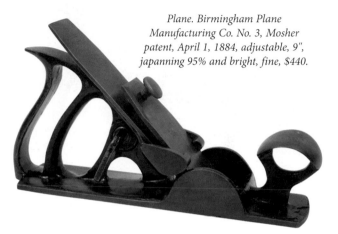

Plane. Bridge Tool Co., No. 2 size, corrugated, minor pitting on blade and body, good **$412**

Plane. E.W. Carpenter, coffin smoother, double wedge, 8", good **$286**

Plane. E.W. Carpenter patent, March 27, 1849, double wedges adjust cutter, 22", perfect tote, good+ **$60**

Plane. E.W. Carpenter No. 2,, Lancaster, Pa., patented, fenced-plank tongue, match, split iron, adjustable-width

Plane. Foss patent, non-adjustable smoother, Stanley blade, Foss cap iron, japanning 85%, good+, $137.

Plane. Birmingham Plane Co., patented, oval body, 4", cutter marked, japanning 75%, good+, $176.

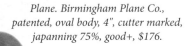

*Plane. L. Bailey, Boston, patented, Aug. 7, 1855, vertical post
Aug. 31, 1858, No. 4 size, japanning 65%, good, $2,310.*

Plane. Blandin patent, May 7, 1867, date marked on base adjuster wheel, No. 7 size, rocker-type adjustment w/ vertical adjuster, japanning 90%, good+, $2,640.

cutting iron sets thickness of tongue, double boxed, marked, good...**$88**

Plane. H. Chapin No. 239 3/4, Solon Rust patent, apple wood, three arms, cast-iron bridle, third-arm steel screw adjustment, refinished, good.................................. **$2,530**

Plane. O.R. Chaplin No. 1, low-angle smoother, patented, No. 1 mark on bed and frog, owner stamp "F.J. Breed, Lynn, Mass." on blade, low blade angle required sides be reworked to make room for cap, handle redesigned to make room for fingers, 7", cutter 1 7/16", plating on metal handles 35%, japanning worn, good+ except for finish **$21,450**

Plane. Consolidated Tool Co. Pilot, low-angle block, lever on cap locks under cap and holds it in place w/ cam, good **$181**

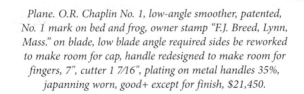

Plane. O.R. Chaplin No. 1, low-angle smoother, patented, No. 1 mark on bed and frog, owner stamp "F.J. Breed, Lynn, Mass." on blade, low blade angle required sides be reworked to make room for cap, handle redesigned to make room for fingers, 7", cutter 1 7/16", plating on metal handles 35%, japanning worn, good+ except for finish, $21,450.

Plane. Consolidated Tool Co. Pilot, low-angle block, lever on cap locks under cap and holds it in place w/ cam, good, $181.

Plane. Copeland & Co., multiform, patented, May 27, 1856, bolt on side and tail of plane controls cutter, cap iron screw adjusts w/ bolt on top of cap, good...........**$77**

Plane. Davis, jack, patented, tote has lost some edge, Mathieson iron, japanning 50%, good......................**$440**

Plane. Duval patent, Nov. 23, 1869, adjustable dado, unmarked, good..**$275**

Plane. Eclipse Plane Co., Coshocton, Ohio, patented, Nov. 24, 1874, adjustable-angle scraper, painted base, original plating 90%, good+ **$770**

Plane. Eclipse Plane Co., Coshocton, Ohio, patented, Nov. 24, 1874, adjustable-angle scraper, little original finish, good **$440**

Plane. Franklin patent, marked, shoe, top edge off tote, japanning 90%, good...**$88**

Plane. Duval patent, Nov. 23, 1869, adjustable dado, unmarked, good, $275.

Plane. L. Bailey, Boston, patented Aug. 7, 1855, vertical post Aug. 31, 1858, No. 3 size, Moulson iron, deep pitting on back, japanning 75%, good, $660.

Plane. Possibly 16th century, iron, dovetailed, round overhanging ends, turned-up nose, wood wedge, file-decorated keeper, good+, $1,430.

Plane. Stanley No. 42, Miller patent, hook type, oval trademark, perfect tote, filletster bed missing nicker, japanning 90%, good+, $18,150.

Plane. Eclipse Plane Co., Coshocton, Ohio, patented, Nov. 24, 1874, adjustable-angle scraper, painted base, original plating 90%, good+, $770.

Plane. Fulton, No. 2 size, much original finish, some original decal on tote, japanning 98%, fine..............**$148**

Plane. Gage No. 1, small size, self-setting, overhanging tote, japanning 90%, good+..**$192**

Plane. Gage No. 2, apple wood, self-setting, tight crack in tote, japanning 92%, good+..**$77**

Plane. Gage No. 4, patented, self-setting, japanning 97%, fine **$187**

Plane. Gerfschaaf (Dutch), late 18th or early 19th century, carved horn, tote, and mouth, 24 1/2", some worm, no iron or wedge, good **$99**

Plane. Gladwin patent, rosewood, two tools, fine **$440**

Plane. Gladwin tool handle, patented, April 18, 1878, japanning 60%, good **$126**

Plane. Harris patent, Sept. 18, 1855, screw adjusts cap iron to cutter, Israel O. Beattie wood jointer, 22", good **$176**

Plane. Hibbard, No. 2 size, japanning 95%, fine **$286**

Plane. Gladwin patent, rosewood, two tools, fine, $440.

Plane. Hollowing, patented, cast iron, round rodlike sole, brass screw cap, open-work handle, japanning 75%, good+.. **$357**

Plane. Gladwin tool handle, patented, April 18, 1878, japanning 60%, good, $126.

Plane. Keen Kutter No. K2, No. 2 size, japanning 95%, fine **$385**

Plane. D. Kimberley patent, three-arm adjustable filletster sash, center iron screw adjusts fence, no handle, adjusting key, repainted iron bridle, good+ **$192**

Plane. D. Kimberley patent, three-arm adjustable plow, center iron screw adjusts fence, handled, overhanging skate, adjusting key, good+.. **$308**

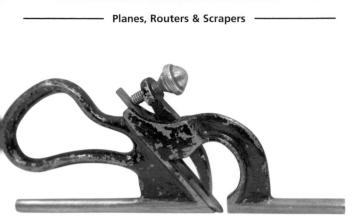

Plane. Hollowing, patented, cast iron, round rodlike sole, brass screw cap, open-work handle, japanning 75%, good+, $357.

Plane. Knowles patent, early 19th century, smoother, No. 2 size, no front knob or handle, winglike sides, overhanging tote, 7 1/4", iron 2 1/8", possibly unique, fine **$2,200**

Plane. Knowles type, unmarked but matches Savage planes, cast-iron body, handles and wedge laminated from light and dark woods, tote end rounded, 9", good **$105**

Plane. Lie-Nielsen No. 9, type 2, mitre, bronze, Stanley style adjuster, wood infill, side handle, original box, new, fine **$797**

Plane. Knowles patent, early 19th century, smoother, No. 2 size, no front knob or handle, winglike sides, overhanging tote, 7 1/4", iron 2 1/8", possibly unique, fine, $2,200.

Plane. Knowles type, unmarked but matches Savage planes, cast-iron body, handles and wedge laminated from light and dark woods, tote end rounded, 9", good, $105.

Plane. Logan & Kennedy, Pittsburgh, patented, similar to Sanford patent, Nov. 26, 1844, coffin smoother, beech, Logan mark on tail, good **$1,100**

Plane. Lowell Plane Co., No. 2 size, Worrall patent, wood bottom w/ bolt at tail to hold iron, 7 1/2", good **$577**

Plane. Mayo, boss, probably presentation piece, plated engraved nuts, plated rod, gold paint decorated w/ red, black, and bright gold detailing, rosewood tote, long and short fence, six cutters, paint 80%, good+ **$1,870**

Plane. Metallic Plane Co., patented, adjustable filletster, later type w/ screws on both ends, most of original length on marked cutter, complete, stress crack at one rivet on tote, japanning 90%, good+ **$1,980**

Plane. Metallic Plane Co., patented, adjustable filletster, dovetailed fence locks in place w/ single screw at end,

Plane. Mayo, boss, probably presentation piece, plated engraved nuts, plated rod, gold paint decorated w/ red, black, and bright gold detailing, rosewood tote, long and short fence, six cutters, paint 80%, good+, $1,870.

Plane. L. Bailey, Boston, patented, Aug. 7, 1855, vertical post Aug. 31, 1858, No. 3 size, iron stamped, japanning 75%, good, $5,060.

tote nearly perfect, small edge chip, shrinkage crack at one rivet, japanning 85%, good+ **$3,850**

Plane. Metallic Plane Co., patented, adjustable filletster, tote complete, marked cutter, japanning 50%, good+ **$1,760**

Plane. Metallic Plane Co., patented, 20", adjustable mouth, corrugated sole, single-wheel adjustment, japanning 50%, good.. **$176**

Plane. Metallic Plane Co., No. 4 size, Palmer & Storkes patent, early triple-lever adjustment, adjustable mouth, corrugated sole, good...**$220**

Plane. Metallic Plane Co., Palmer & Storkes patent, single lever adjuster, marked "Metallic Plane" on side, marked "Ohio Tool Co." on iron, cast-iron knob, adjustable mouth, appears original, japanning worn, good.....**$247**

Plane. ML try plane, dated 1835, maple, iron strike button, carved handle front and back, two horn grips, 47", good+...**$308**

Plane. Muehl patent, Nov. 22, 1904, smoother, buckeye, adjuster on top of blade and part of level cap,

Plane. Metallic Plane Co., patented, adjustable filletster, later type w/ screws on both ends, most of original length on marked cutter, complete, stress crack at one rivet on tote, japanning 90%, good+, $1,980.

corrugated, hairline crack in base of tote, japanning 65%, good+ **$105**

Plane. Multiform molding plane, patented, Aug. 29, 1854, ogee, bevel w/ handle, replacement wedge, 2 7/8" wide, good **$198**

Plane. Metallic Plane Co., patented, adjustable filletster, dovetailed fence locks in place w/ single screw at end, tote nearly perfect, small edge chip, shrinkage crack at one rivet, japanning 85%, good+, $3,850.

Plane. Ohio Tool Co., coffin smoother, Kellett patent, Sept. 16, 1884, three-piece iron, good+ **$44**

Plane. Ohio Tool Co., patented, cast-iron fence, brass rods, adjustable fenced round, double-locking nuts, good+..**$82**

Plane. Ohio Tool Co., smoother, Morris patent, Nov. 8, 1870, proper iron, diamond-pattern sole, tote overhangs

Plane. Boston Metallic Plane Co., smoother, No. 4 size, patented, four-leaf-clover design on cap, Stanley blade, good+, $1,210.

back of body (improved handle design), handle probably original, sides of plane eased at about 45 degrees, 9 1/2", iron 2 1/4", good+.......................... **$1,155**

Plane. "The Phillips Plough Plane Co. Boston. Patented Aug. 31, 1867. Cast by the Metallic Compression Casting Co. No. 46 Congress St. Boston" engraved on skate, rosewood, bronze, three known, probably special casting manufactured for presentation, fine **$39,600**

Plane. Ohio Tool Co., smoother, Morris patent, Nov. 8, 1870, proper iron, diamond-pattern sole, tote overhangs back of body (improved handle design), handle probably original, sides of plane eased at about 45 degrees, 9 1/2", iron 2 1/4", good+, $1,155.

Plane. Brattleboro Tool Co., Steer patent, flower-petal design on cap, unmarked blade possibly replacement, japanning 85%, good+, $154.

Plane. I. Reeder, patent date mark on side, Aug. 2, 1881, one hand, compassed sole, japanning 45%, good+ **$467**

Plane. Probably Leon Robbins, unmarked, laminated from more than 20 pieces of wood, fine.................... **$203**

Plane. Roger patent, Sept. 19, 1882, mitre, double-skew irons, cast-iron table can be set for left and right mitres, complete, repainted, fine... **$825**

Plane. Sandusky Tool Co., smoother, Morris patent, Nov. 8, 1870, date marked in front of wedge, diamond-

Plane. Birdsill Holly, smoother, C. Hott iron, cutter 2" wide, body smooth sole, 9", rosewood tote dovetailed to body, good+, $880.

patterned bottom, 10", unmarked iron 2", much original finish, japanning 90%, fine **$3,960**

Plane. Sandusky Tool Co., grasshopper, cuts two narrow grooves for weather stripping or bell wire, good

.... **$165**

Plane. Sargent No. 707 VBM auto set, No. 2 size, blade marked, corrugated, japanning 94%, good+ **$3,080**

Plane. Siegley No. 7, patented, Stanley Model Shop No. 3803, new, some roughness on tote tip, fine **$137**

*Plane. "The Phillips Plough Plane Co. Boston. Patented
Aug. 31, 1867. Cast by the Metallic Compression Casting
Co. No. 46 Congress St. Boston" engraved on skate,
rosewood, bronze, three known, probably special casting
manufactured for presentation, fine, $39,600.*

Plane. Sargent Lady Bug No. 1507, patented, couple of
mouth chips, plating 85%, good **$440**

Plane. W.C. Scott, Cincinnati, Ohio, end wood and mitre,
cast-brass body, rosewood infill, good+ **$742**

Plane. Otis A. Smith, Fales patent, April 1, 1884,
rosewood handle, fence, 14 matched pairs of bottoms,
no cutters, japanning 75%, good **$275**

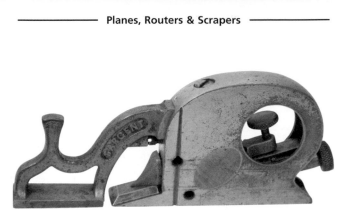

Plane. Sargent Lady Bug No. 1507, patented, couple of mouth chips, plating 85%, good, $440.

Plane. Otis A. Smith, Fales patent, April 1, 1884, rosewood handle, set of bottoms, cutters for two sets of hollows and rounds, three rounds, one hollow, V cut, flat, eight side beads, five center beads, two coves, other miscellaneous attachments, good+ **$880**

Plane. Standard Rule Co. No 21, block, wood body, rosewood knob, cap w/ brass wheel and brass wheel adjustment, replacement blade, 7", good................. **$550**

Plane. Stanley, experimental, based on steel No. 5, converted to adjustable pitch angle, handle slid back, pivoting frog installed, sides reinforced, frog adjusts from 30 to 65 degrees, japanning 97%, fine......... **$1,210**

Plane. W.C. Scott, Cincinnati, Ohio, end wood and mitre, cast-brass body, rosewood infill, good+, $742.

Plane. Stanley, prototype, patented, 1876, No. 1 size, probably made for 1876 U.S. Centennial celebration, lever adjuster as used on Liberty Bell planes, oblong rear tote mounted on vertical cast-iron post, front knob held w/ cast-in steel screw, japanning 97%, fine.......... **$7,920**

Plane. Stanley No. 1, c. 1910, replacement tote, original box w/ some wear, label 95%, good **$1,540**

Plane. Stanley No. 1, second Sweet Hart, No. 1 size, japanning 92%, good+ **$990**

Plane. Stanley No. 2, No. 2 size, long type, blue finish, replacement tote, paint 85%, good **$275**

Plane. Stanley No. 2C, No. 2 size, c. 1915, corrugated, japanning 96%, fine **$357**

Plane. Stanley No. 41, Miller patent, type 3, filletster bed, wraparound fence, japanning 85%, good+ **$880**

Plane. Stanley No. 41, Miller patent, slitter, filletster bed, two-hole fence, six cutters, japanning 94%, fine **$770**

Plane. Stanley No. 42, Miller patent, gunmetal, eight cutters, japanning 97%, fine **$4,125**

Plane. Stanley No. 43, type 2, Miller patent, chip off edge of tote, japanning 55%, good...................................... **$412**

Plane. I. Reeder, patent date mark on side, Aug. 2, 1881, one hand, compassed sole, japanning 45%, good+, $467.

Plane. Stanley No. 141, c. 1900, one cutter, both nose pieces, filletster bed, plating 93%, good+ **$825**

Plane. Stanley No. 141, Sweet Hart, Miller patent, two stops, both nose pieces, eight cutters in wood case, plating 98%, fine **$632**

Plane. Stanley No. 143, Sweet Hart, Miller patent, last type marked 143 on side, both nose pieces, eight cutters in wood case, plating 98%, fine+ **$962**

Plane. Stanley Bed Rock No. 7, type 1, japanning 75%, good+ **$88**

Plane. Stanley, experimental, based on steel No. 5, converted to adjustable pitch angle, handle slid back, pivoting frog installed, sides reinforced, frog adjusts from 30 to 65 degrees, japanning 97%, fine, $1,210.

Plane. Hazzard Knowles patent, 1827, polished cast-iron finish, laminated front knob, inlaid circle of wood on wedge matches knob, single D.R. Barton iron, fine, $2,310.

Plane. Stanley Bed Rock No. 602, type 6, Bed Rock cap, much original finish, japanning nearly 100%, fine
.... **$880**

Plane. Stanley Bed Rock No. 603, type 5, Bed Rock cap, much original finish, japanning nearly 100%, fine
.... **$242**

Plane. Stanley Bed Rock No. 603, type 10, japanning 99%, fine **$302**

Plane. Stanley Bed Rock No. 604, type 4, Bed Rock cap, japanning 92%, fine.. **$88**

Plane. Knowles patent, Savage type, 20", replacement wedge, original green finish 90%, good+, $2,090.

Plane. Stanley Bed Rock No. 604, type 6, corrugated bottom, japanning 80%, good **$100**

Plane. Stanley Bed Rock No. 604 1/2, c. 1925, tote decal 75%, japanning 97%, fine **$330**

Plane. Stanley Bed Rock No. 604 1/2, type 3, S.L.&R. cap, japanning 98%, fine+ **$467**

Plane. Stanley Bed Rock No. 604 1/2C, type 6, corrugated, tote decal 85%, japanning 90% and touched up, good+ **$385**

Plane. Stanley Bed Rock No. 605, type 1, marked "No. 5", S.L.&R. cap, small nick on tote, japanning 85%, good **$110**

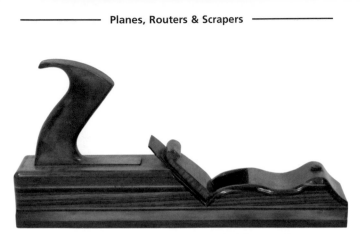

Plane. Probably Leon Robbins, unmarked, laminated from more than 20 pieces of wood, fine, $203.

Plane. Stanley Bed Rock No. 605 1/4, Sweet Hart, japanning 98%, fine **$495**
Plane. Stanley Bed Rock No. 606, type 1, marked "No. 6", S.L.&R. cap, japanning 50%, good **$143**
Plane. Stanley Bed Rock No. 606C, type 7, corrugated, japanning 90%, good+ **$148**
Plane. Stanley Bed Rock No. 607C, type 6, corrugated, japanning 80%, good+ **$154**

Plane. Stanley Bed Rock No. 608, type 3, japanning 96%, fine **$214**

Plane. Stanley Bed Rock No. 608C, type 8, japanning 96%, fine.. **$258**

Plane. Sandusky Tool Co., smoother, Morris patent,
Nov. 8, 1870, date marked in front of wedge,
diamond-patterned bottom, 10", unmarked iron 2",
much original finish, japanning 90%, fine, $3,960.

Plane. Steer patent, Jan. 6, 1885, cutter marked "C.E. Jennings" (early retailer), rosewood strips chipped on nose, tote has crack, japanning 90%, good **$220**

Plane. C. Tollner, 209 Bowery, New York, mitre, marked in two places, probably made in New York City for

Plane. Stanley, prototype, patented, 1876, No. 1 size, probably made for 1876 U.S. Centennial celebration, lever adjuster as used on Liberty Bell planes, oblong rear tote mounted on vertical cast-iron post, front knob held w/ cast-in steel screw, japanning 97%, fine, $7,920.

Tollner, dovetailed body, rosewood infill, 3 3/8", cutter 7/8", good.. **$2,530**

Plane. Tower & Lyon, Chapin patent No. 79, wood bottom, japanning and plating about 95%, fine...... **$550**

Plane. Stanley No. 42, Miller patent, gunmetal, eight cutters, japanning 97%, fine, $4,125.

Plane. Union No. X21, vertical post adjustment, japanning 70%, good.. **$506**

Plane. E. Walker Tool Co., patented, May 19, 1885, multiple skates adjust vertically to match cutter profile, complete, 15 original double-ended cutters, tip off top of tote, good.. **$2,310**

Plane. C. Tollner, 209 Bowery, New York, mitre, marked in two places, probably made in New York City for Tollner, dovetailed body, rosewood infill, 3 3/8", cutter 7/8", good, $2,530.

Plane. Weyland patent, Sept. 27, 1904, made from Stanley No. 4 1/2, self-oiling, fill hole at top of knob, dispensing hole on sole, japanning 90%, good+ **$412**

Plane attachments. For Stanley No. 45, hollow, rounds, and nosing device, early type, no slot for adjuster cutters marked w/ patent date, japanning averages 95%, fine **$495**

Plane. E. Walker Tool Co., patented, May 19, 1885, multiple skates adjust vertically to match cutter profile, complete, 15 original double-ended cutters, tip off top of tote, good, $2,310.

Plow plane. Auburn Tool Co., rosewood, handled, screw arm, minor chips on threads, poly recoated, good+
.... **$385**

Plow plane. Eayrs & Co., Nashua, N.H., beech body, rosewood arms, fence, and wedge, screw arm, no handle, coarse threads, few chips, good+, $335.

*Plow plane. Auburn Tool Co. No. 99,
ebony, two ivory tips, boxwood arms and
nuts, screw arm, chip off tail of fence,
couple thread chips, good, $825.*

Plow plane. Auburn Tool Co. No. 90 1/2, beech,
handled, screw arm, few chips on threads, fine
.... **$165**

Plow plane. Auburn Tool Co. No. 96, boxwood,
improved model w/ turned tips on arms, handled, screw
arm, few chips on threads, good+ **$192**

Plow plane. Babson & Rapplier, Boston, Phillips
improved model, much original finish on tote, black
japanning 96% w/ most of red, blue, and gold highlights
showing, fine **$3,300**

Plow plane. Babson & Rapplier, Boston, Phillips improved model, much original finish on tote, black japanning 96% w/ most of red, blue, and gold highlights showing, fine, $3,300.

Plow plane. E.&A. Baldwin, New York, beech, boxwood arms, handled, screw arm, eight irons, good+ **$247**

Plow plane. Bensen & Crannell, beech, boxwood arms, screw arm, minor chips on top of wedge, fine **$192**

Plow plane. Wm. Blair & Co., Chicago, boxwood, screw arm, few chips, good+... **$236**

Plow plane. E.W. Carpenter, Lancaster, Pa., improved arms patent, boxwood, boxwood arms, rosewood

Plow plane. E.W. Carpenter, Lancaster, Pa., improved arms patent, boxwood, boxwood arms, rosewood nuts, washers, and fence support, knob at end of arms turns to set fence, double lock nuts hold in place, fence support dovetailed to boxwood facing, some roughness on wedge, few chips, good+, $2,090.

nuts, washers, and fence support, knob at end of arms turns to set fence, double lock nuts hold in place, fence support dovetailed to boxwood facing, some roughness on wedge, few chips, good+ **$2,090**

Plow plane. Casey & Kitchell, Auburn, N.Y., beech, screw arm, good **$60**

Plow plane. H. Chapin No. 236 1/2, Rust patent, March 3, 1868, beech, adjustable, three steel arms, steel adjustment screws, good+ **$1,210**

Plow plane. S. Dean, yellow birch, wedge lock,
replacement arm wedges, arm repaired, good, $60.

Plow plane. J. Denson, boxwood, screw arm, eight irons, good+, $385.

Plow plane. H. Chapin No. 239 1/2, tiger-striped apple wood, skate in front of iron extends 2" beyond body, interchangeable sole, small piece off nose of fence boxing, some tapping on wedge, good+ **$1,155**

Plow plane. H. Chapin No. 240 1/2, dark rosewood, handled, screw arm, minor chips on threads, good+ **$495**

Plow plane. G.W. Denison & Co., Winthrop, Conn., rosewood, boxwood arms and nuts, screw arm, handled, couple of minor chips, fine, $825.

Plow plane. Codman patent, maker mark unreadable, ivory scales inlaid in arms fully readable, little yellowing, locking wedge, good+ **$357**

Plow plane. D. Colton, beech, handled, screw arm, eight irons, replacement wedge, good **$99**

Plow plane. Hynson & Gormly, rosewood, boxwood fence and arms, extra long screw arms, handled, good+, $605.

Plow plane. M. Copeland, beech, thumbscrew locking, wood stop, wedge nicked, good+ **$93**

Plow plane. F. Dallicker, A mark, screw arm, missing one screw in stop, wedge beat up, good **$71**

Plow plane. S. Dean, yellow birch, wedge lock, replacement arm wedges, arm repaired, good............**$60**

Plow plane. J. Denson, boxwood, screw arm, eight irons, good+..**$385**

Plow plane. E.H. Morris patent, March 31, 1871, offered in 1887 Sandusky Tool Co. catalog, rosewood handle, scissor-arm mechanism keeps fence and skate parallel, japanning on fence 65%, good+, $1,760.

Plow plane. Auburn Tool Co., rosewood, boxwood arms, handled, screw arm, fine, $462.

Plow plane. J. Denson, boxwood, dark and even patina, minor chipping on screw arm, good............................**$99**

Plow plane. G.W. Denison & Co., Winthrop, Conn., rosewood, boxwood arms and nuts, screw arm, handled, couple of minor chips, fine..**$825**

Plow plane. Eayrs & Co., Nashua, N.H., beech body, rosewood arms, fence, and wedge, screw arm, no handle, coarse threads, few chips, good+.................**$335**

Plow plane. Edgerton, Buffalo, beech, wedge arm, four brass tips, fine...**$115**

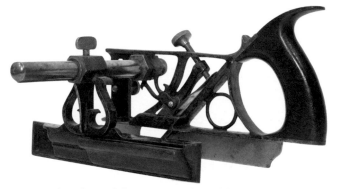

Plow plane. Phillips, type 1, earliest Phillips production, no markings, no boss on frame at cutter-locking screw, two stops, japanning 75%, good+, $1,760.

Plow plane. Hynson & Gormly, rosewood, boxwood fence and arms, extra long screw arms, handled, good+. **$605**

Plow plane. J. Killam, beech, thumbscrew locking, extra long arms, good+ **$110**

Plow plane. D. Kimberly, beech, three arms, steel center screw adjusts fence, handled, slipper-foot toe on skate, original key, metal support for rods painted, good+ **$330**

Plow plane. Sandusky Tool Co., E.H. Morris patent, March 31, 1871, scissor mechanism keeps fence and skate parallel, japanning 65%, good+, $3,850.

Plow plane. I.A. King, probably American, heavy course-threaded arms, steel stop w/ heart-shaped thumbscrew, good..**$319**

Plow plane. S. King, Yankee style, beech, thumbscrew lock, wood stop, good **$330**

Plow plane. E.W. Carpenter, Lancaster, Pa., beech, screw arm, brass stop, few thread chips, good, $275.

Plow plane. A.W. Mack, fruitwood, screw arm, brass stop, unique nut design, threads nearly perfect, fine **$1,430**

Plow plane. E.H. Morris patent, March 31, 1871, offered in 1887 Sandusky Tool Co. catalog, rosewood handle, scissor-arm mechanism keeps fence and skate parallel, japanning on fence 65%, good+ **$1,760**

Plow plane. E.W. Carpenter, Lancaster, Pa., patented, "J. Martien" owner stamp, beech, rosewood edge, improved arms adjust and lock fence in place, good+, $2,640.

Plow plane. Ohio Tool Co., boxwood, set of seven Ohio Tool irons plus one replacement, handled, four ivory tips, good+ **$770**

Plow plane. Ohio Tool Co. No. 57, filletster, beech, fenced, screw arm, double knickers, stopped, couple of thread chips, good+ **$77**

Plow plane. Stanley No. 42, Miller patent, type 1, hook, oval trademark, gunmetal, one cutter, tote perfect, filletster bed missing slitter, japanning 99%, fine, $22,550.

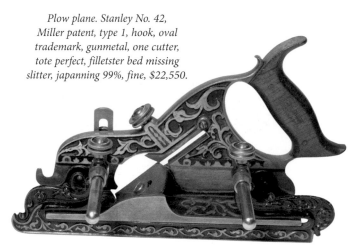

Plow plane. Ohio Tool Co. No. 105, marked, boxwood, applied steel wear plate on fence, handled, four ivory tips, screw arm, weak stamp, even patina, couple of thread chips, good+ **$440**

Plow plane. Ohio Tool Co. No. 105, number mark only, boxwood, four ivory tips, handled, good **$440**

Plow plane. Ohio Tool Co. No. 107B, profile stamp, possibly apple wood, handled, screw arm, much original finish, few chips on threads, good+ **$286**

*Plow plane. Auburn Tool Co. No. 92,
screw arm, handled, fine, $214.*

Plow plane. W. Oothoudt, wedge arm, wood stop,
good+...**$220**

Plow plane. Phillips, type 1, earliest Phillips production,
no markings, no boss on frame at cutter-locking screw,
two stops, japanning 75%, good+..........................**$1,760**

Plow plane. P.B. Rider, Bangor, Maine, initials on mark
hard to read but probably P.B., boxwood screw arm, no
handle, eight irons, minor chips on threads, one washer,
good **$165**

Plow plane. Sandusky Tool Co., E.H. Morris patent, March 31, 1871, scissor mechanism keeps fence and skate parallel, japanning 65%, good+ **$3,850**

Plow plane. J. Schauer, beech, brass top, wedge lock, good **$220**

Plow plane. N. Schauer, beech, brass stop, wedge lock, good **$264**

Plow plane. L. Scovill, thumbscrew locking, wood stop, silver off nose of fence, good **$71**

Plow plane. Jacob Siegley patent, early type, lever-locking cutter holder, set of 15 cutters, long rods, two stops, plating 90% and bright, japanning nearly 90%, fine **$302**

Plow plane. Jacob Siegley, patented, Feb. 10, 1891, "No. 2" cast on fence, set of six cutters in wood box, long rods, two stops, plating worn, japanning nearly 90%, good **$220**

Plow plane. Slaughter C&C, Louisville, Ky., boxwood, screw arm, some thread chips and wedge dings, good **$302**

Plow plane. I. Sleeper, thumbscrews lock arms, wood stop, good **$192**

Plow plane. Stanley No. 41, Miller patent, oval trademark, type 1, hook at top of handle, straight fence, one cutter stop, rods, tote tips rough, japanning about 85%, good.. **$2,200**

Plow plane. Stanley No. 42, Miller patent, type 1, hook, oval trademark, gunmetal, one cutter, tote perfect, filletster bed missing slitter, japanning 99%, fine **$22,550**

Plow plane. Stanley No. 44, Miller patent, pre-slitter type, gunmetal, 12 cutters, some pitting on rear of skate, tote tip narrowed at point, good............................ **$2,860**

Plow plane. Stothert, brass screws at ends of each arm adjust fence, wedge lock, James Cam iron, early item in development of plow, good **$440**

Plow plane. "T.I.", early American, probably fruitwood, handwrought iron depth stop adjusts by turning thumbscrew on top, good..**$137**

Plow plane. H. Lovejoy, Wayne, Maine, eagle stamp, screw arm, wood stop, thumbscrew locking, good **$385**

Plow, beading, and matching plane. Stanley No. 50, new, 17 cutters in wood case, original box taped inside, fine+..**$220**

Prototype plane. Stanley No. 86, side rabbet, "Stanley" and "No. 86" cast into body, forerunner to Stanley No. 79 but slightly smaller, handmade hold-downs and screws, fine..**$2,970**

Prototype plane. Stanley No. 4, Sweet Hart, probably an upscale 4A, Ready Edge blade, aluminum body anodized red inside and out, rare T-lever cap patented

Prototype plane. Stanley No. 4, Sweet Hart, probably an upscale 4A, Ready Edge blade, aluminum body anodized red inside and out, rare T-lever cap patented by James Burdick, June 30, 1931, Stanley aluminum tote, rosewood knob, probably unique, previously Ballintine and Curry collections, fine, $2,310.

by James Burdick, June 30, 1931, Stanley aluminum tote, rosewood knob, probably unique, previously Ballintine and Curry collections, fine **$2,310**
Rabbet block plane. Sargent No. 507, open sides, finish 98%, fine.. **$275**

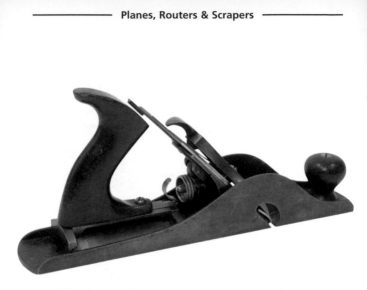

Rabbet plane. Stanley No. 10, R. Hunter patent, April 3, 1906, tote adjustable at three angles to body, triggerlike spring in front of tote locks handle in place, blade worn, japanning 90%, good, $440.

Prototype plane. Stanley No. 86, side rabbet, "Stanley" and "No. 86" cast into body, forerunner to Stanley No. 79 but slightly smaller, handmade hold-downs and screws, fine, $2,970.

Rabbet plane. N. Erlandsen, New York, marked on nose, rosewood wedge, adjustable mouth, cutter worn out, good **$880**

Rabbet plane. Preston patent, adjustable, 1/4" of cutter remains, plating 85%, good **$77**

Rabbet plane. Sargent No. 1506, patented, 3/4" wide, plating nearly 100%, fine **$1,320**

Rabbet plane. Stanley No. 10, mint, original box w/ light edge wear, fine+ **$715**

Rabbet plane. Stanley No. 93, original box worn, fine **$220**

Rabbet plane. Stanley No. 94, Sweet Hart, marked on nose, cutter nearly full, plating 90%, good+ **$275**

Rabbet plane. Stanley No. 196, c. 1908, curved, complete, plating 80%, good **$715**

Rabbet and filletster plane. Sargent No. 79, new, original box, two corners need gluing, fine **$55**

Rabbet and filletster plane. Stanley No. 278, Sweet Hart, decal 90%, original box w/ one edge torn out, fine **$275**

Rabbet and filletster plane. Stanley No. 278, c. 1930, original box worn, label taped, fine+ **$412**

Rabbet plane. Stanley No. 196, curved, script logo, complete, plating 94% but dull, good+, $1,017.

Sash filletster plane. Israel White, beech body and arms, lignum vitae boxing, self-adjusting nuts, two arms, nuts captive to body and adjust fence as turned, skew iron, good+, $2,090.

Sash filletster plane. Israel White, beech body and arms, lignum vitae boxing, self-adjusting nuts, two arms, nuts captive to body and adjust fence as turned, skew iron, good+ **$2,090**

Scraper plane. Stanley No. 12, c. 1900, marked toothing blade, 32 teeth per inch, japanning 90%, good+ **$192**

Scraper plane. Stanley No. 12, Sweet Hart, original box, some label lettering gone, fine **$357**

Scraper plane. Stanley No. 85, Sweet Hart, marked blade, trace of decal on handle, japanning 98%, fine, $687.

*Scraper plane. Stanley No. 85, Sweet Hart, earlier
type marked "Pat. Apl'd for" and "Pat 4-11-05",
marked blade, japanning 95%, fine, $687.*

Scraper plane. Stanley No. 87, unmarked but proper blade, light pitting, japanning 90%, good, $1,100.

Scraper plane. Stanley No. 12 1/4, Sweet Hart, original marked blade, japanning 90%, good+ **$247**

Scraper plane. Stanley No. 12, type 1, 1858 patent-date mark on adjuster wheel, marked blade, japanning 80%, good **$154**

Scraper plane. Stanley No. 12, B casting, marked cutter, japanning 95%, good+ **$88**

Scraper plane. Stanley No. 12 1/4, marked blade, japanning redone, good **$302**

Scraper plane. Stanley No. 85, Sweet Hart, marked blade, few paint spots, japanning 90%, good+ **$605**

Scraper plane. Stanley No. 85, Sweet Hart, marked blade, trace of decal on handle, japanning 98%, fine **$687**

Scraper plane. Stanley No. 85, Model Shop No. 429, shop number marked in four places, rosewood sole fitted to bottom and held in place w/ four screws, unmarked blade probably reject, japanning 90%, good+, $55.

Scraper plane. Stanley No. 85, Model Shop No. 429, shop number marked in four places, rosewood sole fitted to bottom and held in place w/ four screws, unmarked blade probably reject, japanning 90%, good+ **$55**

Scrub plane. Stanley No. 40, rosewood handles, new, original box, fine **$192**

Scraper plane. Stanley No. 87, patent-applied-for type, blade marked but seems thick, japanning 85%, good+, $1,045.

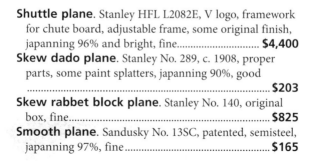

*Shuttle plane. Stanley HFL L2082E,
V logo, framework for chute board,
adjustable frame, some original finish,
japanning 96% and bright, fine, $4,400.*

Shuttle plane. Stanley HFL L2082E, V logo, framework
for chute board, adjustable frame, some original finish,
japanning 96% and bright, fine............................. **$4,400**
Skew dado plane. Stanley No. 289, c. 1908, proper
parts, some paint splatters, japanning 90%, good
.... **$203**
Skew rabbet block plane. Stanley No. 140, original
box, fine.. **$825**
Smooth plane. Sandusky No. 13SC, patented, semisteel,
japanning 97%, fine.. **$165**

Skew dado plane. Stanley No. 289, c. 1908, proper parts, some paint splatters, japanning 90%, good, $203.

Smooth plane. Stanley No. 4S, Sweet Hart, steel body, red-background cap, tote decal about 60%, japanning 97%, fine..**$137**

Smooth plane. Stanley No. 4S, steel body, new, original box, box label 95%, tape on two corners, fine.........**$302**

Smooth plane. Stanley No. 164, Sweet Hart, low angle, proper blade w/graduations, much original finish, japanning 98%, fine, $2,970.

Smooth plane. Stanley No. 164, Sweet Hart, low angle, proper blade w/graduations, japanning 92%, good, $2,420.

Spill plane. Cast iron, cutter held w/lever-locking cam, bronze paint about 95%, good+, $2,530.

Specialty plane. Stanley, router, plows a fixed-width groove, deep center skate, similar to No. 71 router, good **$495**

Spelk plane. For making thin strips of wood for baskets and pillboxes, cutter wraps around plane and locks w/ wedge over top, seven handles, good+ **$154**

Spill plane. Mahogany, skew cutter to shave curly spills from soft wood block, good **$88**

Spill plane. Possibly mahogany, vertical blade, side ejection, good+... **$110**

Split-frame shoot-board plane. L. Bailey, patented, Aug. 7, 1855, beech tote, Moulson cutter, early lever cap, no cap iron screw, small chip in rail at nose, two known, good+.. **$5,500**

T rabbet plane. Birmingham Plane Manufacturing Co., low-angle cutter, non-adjustable, japanning 70% and bright, good+, $935.

T rabbet plane. Birmingham Plane Manufacturing Co., low-angle cutter, non-adjustable, japanning 70% and bright, good+.. **$935**

Table planes. Rule joint, no maker mark, probably manufactured, c. 1800, matched set, 10", fine **$247**

Thumb planes. Ibex, set of three, 1" to 2", brass, rounded soles, screw locking cap, fine..................... **$198**

Tonguing and grooving plane. Sargent No. 1068, new, original box covered in tape, fine..................... **$275**

Travisher. Early, 5", cutting edge about 2 1/4", fine
.... **$105**

T rabbet plane. Birmingham Plane Manufacturing Co., 6", iron 1 1/2", japanning 85%, good, $385.

Universal plane. Stanley No. 55, complete, instructions, original box, fine.. **$770**

Veneer scraper. Stanley No. 12, new, original box in pieces, picture label full but dark, fine...................... **$275**

Veneer scraper. Stanley No. 12 3/4, Sweet Hart, marked blade, locking screw, extra thick rosewood sole, japanning 99%, fine... **$1,650**

Veneer scraper. Stanley No. 12 3/4, Sweet Hart, marked blade, locking screw, extra thick rosewood sole, japanning 95%, fine... **$2,310**

Veneer scraper. Stanley No. 12 3/4, Sweet Hart, marked blade, locking screw, extra thick rosewood sole, japanning 95%, fine, $2,310.

Weather-stripping plane. Stanley No. 239 1/8, Sweet Hart, complete, japanning 96%, fine.........................**$148**

Weather-stripping plane. Stanley No. 378, three special stops, two stop collars, japanning 98%, fine **$88**

Wheelwright's felloe plane. Fastens to hub and levels felloes, couple of replacement wedges, good **$264**

Wood scraper. Stanley No. 81, Sweet Hart, original box, fine **$467**

Wooden bottom plane. Bailey No. 5, Boston, smoother, type 1, banjo-lever cap, japanning 55%, good **$550**

Wooden bottom plane. Stanley No. 26, jack, Bailey around nose, nose decal 99%, japanning 99%, fine+, $302.

Wooden bottom plane. Stanley Gage No. G26, japanning 99%, fine+, $275.

Wooden bottom plane. Birmingham Plane Co., 20", cutter 2 3/8", japanning 75%, good **$121**
Wooden bottom plane. Stanley No. 21, smoother, first pre-lateral, japanning 85%, good..............................**$154**
Wooden bottom plane. Stanley No. 22, type 12, much original finish, japanning 96%, fine **$110**
Wooden bottom plane. Stanley No. 24, smoother, long version, Bailey cast around nose, japanning 85%, good
....**$71**

Wooden bottom plane. Stanley No. 25, block, pre-lateral, solid cap, adjuster nut, traces of original finish, japanning 90%, good+ **$275**

Wooden bottom plane. Stanley No. 26, jack, pre-lateral, no number on nose, solid cap, adjuster screw, japanning 65%, good **$16**

Wooden bottom plane. Stanley No. 27 1/2, jack, much original finish, japanning 96%, fine **$82**

Wooden bottom plane. Stanley No. 28, jack, pre-lateral, no number on nose, solid cap, adjuster screw, japanning 85%, good+ **$93**

Wooden bottom plane. Stanley No. 28, jointer, last model, much original finish, japanning 95%, fine **$357**

Wooden bottom plane. Stanley No. 30, jointer, pre-lateral, number on nose, solid cap, adjuster screw, japanning touched up, good **$82**

Wooden bottom plane. Stanley No. 31, jointer, type 6, pre-lateral, japanning 90%, good+ **$115**

Wooden bottom plane. Stanley No. 32, type 4, pre-lateral, traces of original finish, japanning 90%, good+ **$115**

Wooden bottom plane. Stanley No. 33, type 6, pre-lateral, traces of original finish, japanning 93%, good+ **$137**

Wooden bottom plane. Stanley No. 33, jointer, type 13, Bailey around nose, traces of original finish, japanning 94%, good+ **$253**

Wooden bottom plane. Stanley No. 34, type 4, pre-lateral, japanning 93%, good **$38**

Wooden bottom plane. Stanley No. 34, jointer, type 14, Bailey around nose, paint spots, japanning 90%, good+ **$154**

Wooden bottom plane. Stanley No. 37, jenny, Bailey around nose, japanning 85%, good+ **$165**

Wooden bottom plane. Stanley Gage No. G27 1/2, japanning 95%, good+ **$165**

Wooden bottom plane. Stanley Gage No. G28, japanning 95%, good+ **$385**

Wooden bottom plane. Stanley Gage No. G35, japanning 95%, good+ **$115**

Wooden door plane. Ohio Tool Co. No. 139 1/2, double wedge and iron, cuts edge of door stiles to receive panels, good+ **$220**

Wooden plane. Carved dog's-head handle, full detail, good+ **$440**

Wooden plane. Dated 1830, marked "U.S." on iron, probably chestnut, skewed iron 5", body 28", applied fence, top off tote, good+ **$192**

Wooden plane. D. Amsden, Lebanon, N.H., badger, wedged nicker, 22", 4" wide, good **$110**

Wooden plane. Sandusky Tool Co., special coffin smoother, marked on nose and iron, mahogany, narrow body, 9", cutter 1 3⁄8", fine, $742.

Wooden plane. Thomas Appleton, Boston, reeding, four beads, skew cutter, good+ **$137**

Wooden plane. E. Bassett, quarter round, beech, 10", applied and fixed fences, inlaid iron wear plates, good+ **$220**

Wooden plane. I. Bickford, strong rare mark, jointer, heavy flat chamfers, diamond strike button, chip off side of closed tote, good..**$88**

Wooden plane. Router, D type, tiger maple, two pieces joined together for flame or book-matched pattern, scroll ends for handles w/ some carving, good+, $82.

Wooden plane. I. Blosfom, fore, diamond strike button, 21", good+ **$105**

Wooden plane. H. Russell Cabot, Vermont, crown molding starter, A mark, yellow birch, handled, 3" wide, good+ **$93**

Wooden plane. T.C. Cain, Ravenna, dado, 1 1/2" wide, good **$16**

Wooden plane. E.W. Carpenter, Lancaster, bead, handled, boxed, fine **$247**

Wooden plane. Carved dog's-head handle, full detail, good+, $440.

Wooden plane. E.W. Carpenter, Lancaster, beech, screw arm, good...**$385**

Wooden plane. E.W. Carpenter, Lancaster, coffin mitre, 10", good **$181**

Wooden plane. E.W. Carpenter, Lancaster, combination match, cuts groove in one direction and tongue in other, narrow size marked 1/2, good+ **$121**

Wooden plane. Samuel Auxer, Lancaster, Pa., beveling plane, wedge locked, slightly skewed iron, fine, $1,430.

Wooden plane. E. Bassett, bead, boxed, good, $275.

Wooden plane. E.W. Carpenter, Lancaster, crown, handled, fenced, ogee, 5", good.................................. **$154**

Wooden plane. E.W. Carpenter, Lancaster, pilaster, cuts round and three steps, handled, fenced, 5", fine
.... **$550**

Wooden plane. E.W. Carpenter, Lancaster, toothing, 6 1/2", good... **$286**

Wooden plane. E.W. Carpenter, Lancaster, washboard, groove and follower, fine **$412**

Wooden plane. C.E. Chelor, Wrentham, bead, birch, replacement wedge, 10", good.................................... **$495**

Wooden plane. Belection, early 19th century, flat profile, massive wedge appears to be old replacement, good+, $77.

Wooden plane. C.E. Chelor, Wrentham, rabbet reworked to dovetail, yellow birch, 10", good+ **$440**

Wooden plane. Coffin smoother, rosewood, finger and thumb grips wider than plane and carved into sides, minor chips on nose and tail, good+ **$247**

Wooden plane. Collins, Ravenna, A mark, adjustable screw-arm sash, triple boxing, double wedges and irons, good+ **$110**

Wooden plane. Collins, Ravenna, A mark, belection, boxed, 1 13/16" wide, good+ **$71**

Wooden plane. I. Walton, Reading, tongue, possibly birch, 10 1/4", good+, $1,980.

(End view.)

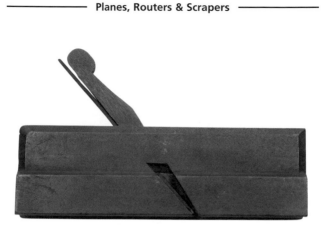

Wooden plane. H. Wetherell, Norton, quarter round, birch, relieved wedge, 9 7/8", nearly full depth, fine, $2,090.

Wooden plane. R.J. Collins, astragal, cove, wide flat chamfers, 2", good **$220**

Wooden plane. R.J. Collins, Ravenna, C mark, Roman ogee, good+... **$105**

Wooden plane. R.J. Collins, Ravenna, C mark w/o location stamp, round, good+.................................... **$110**

Wooden plane. J. Colton, double irons and wedges, ogee, bevel, good+ **$50**

*Wooden plane. Closed tote carved from solid
whalebone and ends w/tail, throat carved w/double
arch, body probably holly, 18", good+, $154.*

Wooden plane. J. Colton, Jones patent, chute board, C
mark, iron frame, 23", good+ **$330**

Wooden plane. S. Doggett, Dedham, hollow, early,
birch, 10 1/4", good **$385**

Wooden plane. Eyers & Co., Nashua, N.H., jointer,
heavy rosewood or cocobolo, 22", minor roughness on
nose, fine **$176**

Wooden plane. Isaac Field, quirk ovolo and astragal,
yellow birch, boxed, good+ **$160**

Wooden plane. C. Fuller, Boston, gothic bead and ogee
mold, handled, boxed, 3 1/4" wide, good+ **$357**

*Wooden plane. Addison Heald,
Milford, N.H., coffin smoother,
rosewood, strike and rosewood
wedge w/streak of sapwood, 4 1/2",
mark a bit weak, good+, $236.*

Wooden plane. Jo. Fuller, Providence, early rare mark, cuts a flat and bevel, yellow birch or possible fruitwood, mouth open but probably not recut, good **$126**

Wooden plane. Greenfield Tool Co., ovolo, bevel, double irons and wedges, boxed, good **$50**

Wooden plane. Sandusky Tool Co., special coffin smoother, marked on nose and iron, mahogany, narrow body, 9", cutter 1 3/8", fine **$742**

Wooden plane. Aaron Upton, sash, beech, good+ **$220**

Wooden plane. T. Waterman, Maine, early, belection, yellow birch, 1 1/8" wide, hang hole in nose, good+ **$330**

Wooden plane. J. Webb, Pittsfield, combination match plane, lignum vitae, crack in one wedge, good **$99**

Wooden plane. H. Wetherell, Middleton, jointer, round top wedge, square strike bottom, 26", good **$71**

Wooden plane. H. Wetherell, Norton, rabbet, birch, both nickers missing, some roughness on tail, good **$220**

Wooden plane. A. Wheaton, Philadelphia, groove, 9 3/4", strong mark, good **$88**

Wooden plane. Charles White, Warren, molder, handled, original applied fence, 3 1/2" wide, good+ **$121**

*Wooden plane. N. Taber, panel raiser, beech,
curved profile, adjustable fence, fixed stop,
round wedge and iron, 14", good+, $495.*

Wooden plane. Jo. Wilbur, early, fluting, 10", good
....**$143**

Wooden plane. Robert Wooding, c. 1700, round, skew
iron, 8 1/8", good **$160**

Wooden plane. Robert Wooding, hollow, 9 7/8", good
....**$137**

Wooden plane. Robert Wooding, round, 10 1/8", good
....**$302**

Wooden plane. H. Yost, Lewisburg, Pa., Roman ogee,
handled, applied fence, good+ **$264**

Wooden planes. E.W. Carpenter, Lancaster, set of plank
match planes, No. 2 size, screw arms, handled, fine
....**$385**

Wooden plane. Router, D type, tiger maple, two pieces
joined together for flame or book-matched pattern,
scroll ends for handles w/ some carving, good+........**$82**

Wooden planes. I. Walton, Reading, 18th century,
hollow and round pair, fruitwood, 10 1/4" long, 1 3/4"
wide, hang hole in tail, good **$797**

Wooden plow plane. A. Smith, Rehoboth, early, beech,
thumbscrew lock, wood stop, pitted skate, wedge a bit
dinged, good..**$77**

Wooden plow plane. A. Smith, warranted, early,
beech, thumbscrew lock, wood stop, relieved wedge,
good+...**$66**

Rules, Squares & Gauges

Although no one knows for certain, it is likely that the first man-made measuring device was a straight stick with notches cut into it. By the time the ancient Egyptians were constructing the Great Pyramids, more refined techniques had evolved, but they still relied on very basic materials such as sticks and cords.

It is known that the Romans were using jointed metal rulers, and more accurate measuring devices continued to evolve in the following centuries. By the Renaissance era, more specialized rulers and measuring devices had become the tools of various trades, such as architecture.

It wasn't until the 18th century that commercial production of rules began, and England was the first country to develop this industry. It continued to be a leading center of production well into the 19th century. American manufacturing began during the first quarter of the 19th century, and by the 1860s automated production of folding rules was under way in this country.

The favored material for rules since the 18th century has been boxwood, often with the sections joined by fittings made of brass or German silver (an alloy). High quality rules were also made from ivory, and these choice examples are much sought after by collectors. The Stanley Rule and Level Company, as the original name implies, became a leader in the production of this tool by the mid-19th century. In the early 20th century, Stanley introduced the multi-hinged "zig-zag" type rule, followed some years later by the steel pull-push tape measure that has remained the favorite style ever since.

Bevel gauge. Howard patent, 1867, rosewood handle w/ level, brass handle ends and side plates, full-length iron top plate, steel blade w/ elongated hole, blade graduated to 7 1/2", good **$170**

Bevel square. Sargent patent, July 22, 1873, Model Shop No. 867, rosewood handle w/ brass trim, much original finish on handle, some bluing on blade, production version had metal handle, fine, $742.

Bevel square. Manufactured, two blades, each has own slot in extra-thick handle, fine, $242.

Bevel square. St. Johnsbury Tool Co., double blades, rosewood and brass handle w/ locking screw in base, blades 6", good, $1,265.

Bevel protractor. Darling, Brown & Sharpe No. 34, adjustable blade pivots around blade w/ protractor, good+...**$82**

Bevel square. Dated 1837, chip carved on both sides, handwrought iron rivet w/ brass washer, blade 14", good **$192**

Bevel square. L. Bailey patent, March 19, 1872, cast-iron handle w/ lever lock at base, 10", good....................**$220**

Bevel square. L.D. Howard patent, Nov. 5, 1867, level in brass-bound rosewood handle, 7", good+................**$231**

Bevel square. L.D. Howard patent, Nov. 5, 1867, cast brass handle w/ level, 8", good+ **$412**

Bevel square. Sargent patent, July 22, 1873, Model Shop No. 867, rosewood handle w/ brass trim, much original finish on handle, some bluing on blade, production version had metal handle, fine.................................. **$742**

Bevel square. S. Towers, brass and rosewood body, manufactured, blade 29", good **$220**

Blacksmith's rule. Lufkin Rule Co., Cleveland, Ohio, steel, two-fold, brass tips, 2', good+ **$50**

Board cane. Stanley No. 48, unmarked, hickory, even patina, nearly straight, good+ **$192**

Board rule. Dated 1816, pewter ends, hand-stamped numbers, eight sides, good **$66**

Board rule. E.M. Chapin, Pine Meadow, Conn., brass ends, strong marks, good+ **$66**

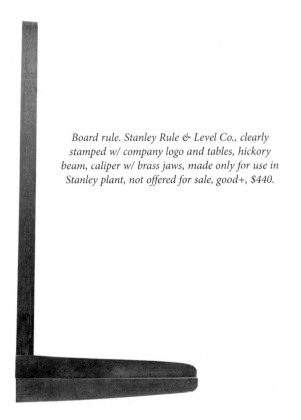

Board rule. Stanley Rule & Level Co., clearly stamped w/ company logo and tables, hickory beam, caliper w/ brass jaws, made only for use in Stanley plant, not offered for sale, good+, $440.

Board rule. Stanley Rule & Level Co., clearly stamped w/ company logo and tables, hickory beam, caliper w/ brass jaws, made only for use in Stanley plant, not offered for sale, good+ **$440**

Board rule. Stanley No. 46, not marked, octagon, brass ends, strong marks, good+ **$60**

Board rule. Stanley No. 46 1/2, not marked, square, brass ends, strong marks, bright, fine **$115**

Board scale. Blackington & Carley, Newport, N.H., advertising item, brass end is board hook, includes tailor's gauging rule by Bellows, brass fittings, 24", finish 97%, good..**$99**

Board scale. A. Frost, eight-sided, alternating layers of light and dark wood, brass cap on one end laid out in feet, covered w/ scales, good+....................................**$110**

Board scale. R.B. Haselton, Contoocook, N.H., brass end is board hook, tally holes, 24", yellow finish 97%, fine **$55**

Board scale. Six brass tally buttons slide in brass track on both edges, scales on top and bottom, readable but faint, good **$132**

Board scale. James Watts, Boston, brass ends, dirty, 24", good+..**$71**

Board stick. G.T. Younglove, Fitchburg, Mass., handle type, brass end, good+ **$170**

Boiler inspector's rule. Stanley, Sweet Hart, marked "H.S.B.I. & I." (Hartford Steam Boiler Inspection & Insurance Co.), special order, good+ **$220**

Boxwood rule. Belcher Brothers, New York, ship carpenter's bevel, double brass blade, even patina, good+ **$71**

Boxwood rule. H. Chapin No. 40, two-fold, 2', board tables, clear markings, fine...**$93**

Boxwood rule. Chapin-Stephens Co., board rule, two-fold, 2', edge marks, good+...**$71**

Boxwood rule. Chapin-Stephens Co., four-fold, 2', board tables inside and out, clean, tight joints, fine **$176**

Boxwood rule. C-S Co. No. 83, four-fold, 2', 6" slide in one leg, broad, traces of original finish on inside, good+ **$110**

Boxwood rule. W. & L.E. Gurley, dry measure rule, for laying out containers for fabrication, table for pints to bushels, some original finish, fine............................. **$286**

Boxwood rule. Hays, improved practical mechanic's rule, four-fold, 3', scales, double-arch joint, steel tips, fine **$66**

Boxwood rule. J. Rabone & Sons No. 1214, iron monger's, three-fold, caliper 1 foot, scales for irons rounds, flats, and more, good **$137**

Boxwood rule. Stanley, marked w/ "Rule & Level Co." trademark and "Special", special rope caliper, wide English type, graduated to 4" in English layout, traces of original finish, fine, $990.

Boxwood rule. J. Rabone & Sons, iron monger's, four-fold, caliper 2', scales for iron rounds, flats, copper, and more, good **$132**

Boxwood rule. John A. Roebling's Sons Co., round top, tables, 4 1/2", good+ **$66**

Boxwood rule. John A. Roebling's Sons Co., ogee end on caliper, tables, 5 1/2", good+ **$242**

Boxwood rule. John A. Roebling's Sons Co., rope caliper w/ tables, good+ **$110**

Boxwood rule. Stanley, advertising for "New Jersey Steel & Iron Co. Bridges, Buildings, Fireproofing", four-fold, outside bevel edges w/ scales, 2', some original finish, fine **$154**

Boxwood rule. Stanley No. 2, two-fold, 2', good+ **$165**

Boxwood rule. Stanley No. 3, four-fold, 1-foot caliper, traces of original finish, good+ **$93**

Boxwood rule. Stanley No. 5, two-fold, 2', fine **$198**

Boxwood rule. Stanley No. 13, caliper, two-fold, 6", good ı **$176**

Boxwood rule. Stanley No. 16, engineer's, two-fold, 2', tables, scales, slide, arch joint, good+ **$357**

Boxwood rule. Stanley No. 22, marked "Stanley Rule & Level", two-fold, 2', board tables, fine **$357**

Boxwood rule. Stanley No. 30, metric, four-fold, 1 meter, English markings on inside, good+ **$577**

Boxwood rule. Stanley No. 31, early type, not marked for shrinkage, strong markings, couple of saw nicks on edge, good+ **$88**

Boxwood rule. Stanley No. 31, later type, marked 1/8" per foot shrinkage, fine.. **$110**

Boxwood rule. Stanley No. 31 1/2E, "In. Per Ft. Shrinkage," two-fold, 2', fine **$132**

Boxwood rule. Stanley No. 32, Sweet Hart, special, English and metric, joints tight, finishes 95%, fine **$220**

Boxwood rule. Stanley No. 32EM, English and metric, joints tight, finish 99%, fine **$550**

Boxwood rule. Stanley No. 35, marked Stanley, narrow caliper, two-fold, 1 foot, 6" long, readable, good **$220**

Boxwood rule. Stanley No. 36 1/2EM, Sweet Hart, English and metric, finish nearly 100%, fine **$352**

Boxwood rule. Stanley No. 51, New Britain logo, metric, four-fold, 2', good+ **$225**

Boxwood rule. Stanley No. 62, E&M metric, Sweet Hart, four-fold, 2', brass bound, much original finish, some tarnish, fine **$132**

Boxwood rule. Stanley No. 66 3/4, Sweet Hart, brass bound, 3', most original finish, fine **$77**

Boxwood rule. Stanley No. 68, E&M metric, Sweet Hart, four-fold, 2', fine **$176**

Boxwood rule. Stanley No. 79, four-fold, 2', board scales, good+ **$137**

Boxwood rule. Stanley No. 83, four-fold, 2', brass slide 6", slight spring when closed, fine **$605**

Boxwood rule. Stanley No. 94, four-fold, 4', brass bound, improved arch joint, fine **$126**

Boxwood rule. A. Stanley,
marked "W.M. Hipple" on back,
two-fold, 2', slide, good+, $742.

Boxwood rule. Stanley No. 98, desk rule, 12", good+
.... **$105**
Boxwood rule. A. Stanley & Co., two-fold, 2', good+
.... **$550**
Boxwood rule. A. Stanley & Co., satinwood, two-fold,
2', slide, gradations scribed in, good **$550**
Boxwood rule. Stanley Rule & Level Co., early, "Jas.
Hogg Improved Slide Rule," "Pat. Applied For," German-
silver bound, slide, tables, good+ **$1,210**

*Butt gauge. Stanley, head has marker
for hinge, double brass screws on head,
one locks head to beam, other locks
butt marker in place, good+, $110.*

Boxwood rule. E.A. Stearns No. 14, Brattleboro, Vt., four-fold, 2', broad, bound, board scaled inside, good+ **$275**

Boxwood rule. Winchester No. 9568, two-fold, 2', fine **$132**

Bridge builder's square. Eagle Square, patented, Jan. 8, 1870, double legs, no cross piece, bright, shiny, fine **$115**

Butt gauge. Henry Plante patent, Feb. 23, 1886, rosewood, dovetailed slide, brass wear plates, good+ **$258**

Butt gauge. Stanley, head has marker for hinge, double brass screws on head, one locks head to beam, other locks butt marker in place, good+ **$110**

Calculating rule. E. Smith & Co., Rockford, Ill., patented, Oct. 24, 1876, extension rule, trammel points, board tables, complete, fine.......................................**$440**

Calculating rule. E.A. Stearns, Brattleboro, Vt., Charles B. Long patent, April 26, 1865, two-fold, 2', covered w/ tables, fully readable, good+......................................**$605**

Caliper. Heavy brass, steel jaws, direct-reading head can be read for inside measure on one side and outside measure on other, good **$66**

Caliper. Livingston Manufacturing Co., Rockland, Maine, heavy brass adjustable jaw slides along 1/2" square beam, scale in inches, good...**$38**

Calipers. W.R. Robertson, miniature, double-acting full-body ladies w/ pointed toes for inside measure and pointed hairstyle for outside, brass, about 1", fine.....**$60**

Chisel-grinding gauge. Stanley No. 200, plating 98%, fine **$55**

Clock maker's traveler. A.A. Adams, 1853, brass wheel graduated and marked on both sides, turned wood handle, fine **$220**

Clock maker's traveler. Five-pointed star, probably handwrought, hard-wood handle, brass ferrule, wheel 4", good..**$132**

Coachbuilder's square. Brass, steel blade adjusts and locks at any angle around full circle, screw locking in tail of handle, good+ **$82**

Combination marking gauge. O. Brown & T.F. Berry, patented, July 7, 1868, six-sided, brass slides on five sides, boxwood set screws lock five slides in place, few chips in slide tracks, good, $3,190.

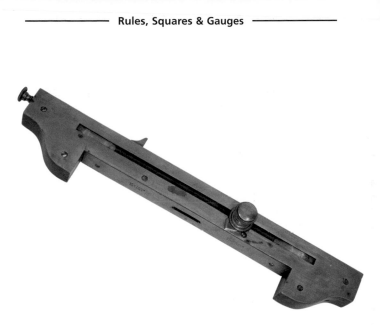

Clapboard gauge. Nester patent, Dec. 31, 1867, brass, mahogany, multifunction, fine, $203.

Combination gauge. Kenny patent, marking, mortise, and trammels, double heads, one in boxwood, one in rosewood, brass beam w/ fixed center point and screw-adjustable points, good+ **$440**

Combination marking gauge. Mortise and slitting, English patent, brass, ebony, good+ **$187**

Combination marking gauge. O. Brown & T.F. Berry, patented, July 7, 1868, six-sided, brass slides on five

Combination gauge. Kenny patent, marking, mortise, and trammels, double heads, one in boxwood, one in rosewood, brass beam w/ fixed center point and screw-adjustable points, good+, $440.

Combination gauge. Otis Smith, Rockford, Conn., two-piece brass rod w/ marking, mortise, and panel, complete, japanning 90%, fine, $770.

sides, boxwood set screws lock five slides in place, few chips in slide tracks, good **$3,190**

Combination rule. Lufkin No. 863L, original box, label 80%, fine.. **$121**

Combination rule. Stephens No. 036, new, original box worn, bottom and full clear top label, fine.............. **$385**

Combination square. P.L. Fox, patented, Oct. 2, 1888, cast-iron try, adjustable bevel and mitre, blade bright, japanning nearly 100%, fine...................................... **$132**

Comparison rule. Nils Lind, 1771, name and date surrounded by crowns and floral cartouches, probably satinwood, compares London, Paris, Stockholm, and Barban scales to 24 units, four-fold, legs about 3/8" square, fine.. **$302**

Cooper's dividers. Elm, double-acting screw, good+ **$110**

Cooper's dividers. Elm, double-acting screw, steel points w/ bone ferrules, good **$198**

Cooper's dividers. Washer under thumbscrew for joint marked "The Lewis & Fowler Manf. Co." (may be reused part), wood, steel points, brass ferrules, 39", good+ **$93**

Cooper's dividers. Wrought iron, 42", missing thumbscrew, good.. **$110**

Cooper's stave gauges. Oak, seven patterns w/ various arcs, graduated for width, good **$192**

Customs gauging-rod jaws. Prime & McKean, wood version of Stanley rod, USS filigree in corners, only known example in wood, no rod, two jaws, fine **$264**

Customs-house rule. J. Watts, Boston, measures barrel length from head to head, good **$121**

Double bevel. Stanley Model Shop No. 2349, marked "A.F. Schade 12.22.1911", blades on both ends, brass plate at center, blades 6" and marked Stanley, fine, $1,540.

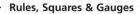

Dividers. Amour's, 18th century, knife joint, some decoration on legs, 24", good+, $110.

Desk rule. D. Webster Clegg, concave ruler and paper cutter, patented, Sept. 10, 1867, brass edges, 18", original price $1.90, much original finish, fine...................... **$105**

Dividers. Amour's, 18th century, knife joint decorated on both sides, 26", good.. **$220**

Dividers. Handwrought, early, fine adjustment, thumbscrew has fancy pigtail-turned ends, 23", good+ **$99**

Dividers. Not marked, brass, steel legs, joint, and arch, 29 1/2", fine.. **$275**

Double bevel. Stanley Model Shop No. 2349, marked "A.F. Schade 12.22.1911", blades on both ends, brass

Dividers. Early, large brass protractor on one leg covered w/ scales, steel tips w/ fancy decoration, good, $308.

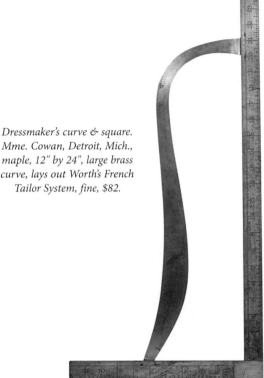

Dressmaker's curve & square. Mme. Cowan, Detroit, Mich., maple, 12" by 24", large brass curve, lays out Worth's French Tailor System, fine, $82.

plate at center, blades 6" and marked Stanley, fine **$1,540**

Double calipers. Dated 1878, marked but not readable, jaws locked in place by thumbscrews, quarter-circle arc, wood handle, good+..**$154**

Double calipers. Early, handwrought, eight-sided shank, round handle w/ button end, hand finished w/ hammer and file, 23", fine **$105**

Double calipers. S.K. Gatchell, early, both legs adjust about the center and can be locked into position by thumbscrews on quarter-circle arc, 29", good **$99**

Double calipers. Handwrought, both legs adjustable and can be locked in position, loop end is hand formed, 19", good+..**$105**

Dressmaker's curve & square. Mme. Cowan, Detroit, Mich., maple, 12" by 24", large brass curve, lays out Worth's French Tailor System, fine..............................**$82**

Dry measure rule. W. & L.E. Gurley, brass bound, four-fold, 2', tables for calculating volume in bushels and parts thereof, some staining, good **$77**

Ebony rule. Not marked, possibly for metric layout, two-fold, brass hinge plates w/ brass tips that end w/ steel plates, 19 3/4", fine..**$198**

Floor gauge. E.W. Carpenter, Lancaster, dovetailed handled, stepped face, good+.......................................**$55**

Floor gauge. Handle dovetailed into curved body, walnut, fine **$27**

Folding measure. Stanley, London, 1890, brass, graduated to 100 by tens, seven fold, sections about 3/8" square, good+ **$280**

Gauge. Barn builder's, walnut, graduated, Roman numerals, early handwrought thumbscrews adjust sliding section, beams end w/ thumbnail moldings, good+ **$165**

Gauge. Bates patent, Oct. 20, 1896, bronze head tilts for bevel edges on one side, other side designed for curved edges, good+ **$126**

Gauge. Stanley No. 60, Traut patent, japanning 80% and enhanced, good **$55**

Gauge. Stanley Rule & Level Co., A. Williams patent, May 26, 1857, full logo w/o eagle trademark, rosewood head, steel wear plate, brass beam, screw adjustable mortise points, good+ **$165**

Gunner's calipers. Brass, graduated to 24", 24" tall, original finish, good+ **$154**

Gunther's scale. Belcher Bros. & Co., New York, maple, brass pins and ends, 2', good+ **$60**

Gunther's scale. Belcher Bros & Co., New York, covered w/ scales front and back, brass pins for setting dividers, fine **$275**

Framing square. Standing eagles, 1843, date and eagle on one side, eagle only on other side, 4" by 6", hand-stamped tapered legs, some pitting, good, $110.

Gauge. Kinney patent, rotary marking, shown in 1885 Sandusky Tool Co. catalog, notched rotating head, good, $495.

*Gauging rod. Stanley No. 45,
table for wine gallons to 120,
two chips on one side, fine, $165.*

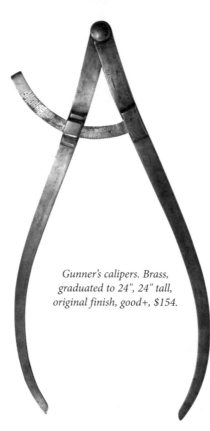

*Gunner's calipers. Brass,
graduated to 24", 24" tall,
original finish, good+, $154.*

Hatter's rule. Ivory, ebony, German-silver trimming, fine **$220**

Head caliper. Belcher Brothers, U.S. standard, maple, brass fittings and corners, good+ **$132**

Height gauge. Starrett No. 454 E & M, 24", original wood box, fine...**$55**

Hoof measure. John Hood Co., Boston, cast-iron base, brass arm, good.. **$126**

Ivory caliper. German-silver fittings and slide, light yellowing, hairline at one end, good **$137**

Ivory rule. Acme Rule Co., caliper, Acme patent, "Pat. Appl'd," wood core, two-fold, 6", ivory scales on sides, light yellowing, good+... **$440**

Ivory rule. Acme Rule Co., caliper, Acme patent, "Pat. Appl'd For", wood core, four-fold, 12", ivory scales on sides, light yellowing, good+ **$302**

Ivory rule. Belcher Brothers & Co., New York, early, four-fold, 2', scales, edge markings, some damage at one hinge including edge chip, good................................. **$170**

Ivory rule. Belcher Brothers, New York, engineer's, two-fold, 2', brass trimmings, ivory slide, scales, tables, edge markings, small chip on leg, two 3/16" hairlines at joint, good+.. **$2,200**

Ivory rule. J. Buck, hinge joint engraved "Presented to Mr. Stephen Palmer by the carpenters ingaged on the works erected by Mess. Wm. Brass & Son at Hanwell as a mark of respect. 1857.", four-fold, 2', German silver, arch joint, slide, scales, tables, edge marks, light yellowing, fine **$660**

Ivory rule. E.M. Chapin No. 60 1/2, architect's, four-fold, 2', German silver, bevel edges, fine **$715**

Ivory rule. E.M. Chapin No. 63, broad, four-fold, 2', German silver, arch joint, edge marked, tobacco yellow, good **$275**

Ivory rule. E.M. Chapin No. 74, caliper, two-fold, 6", white, German-silver bindings and hinge, fine **$302**

Ivory rule. E.M. Chapin No. 77, caliper, four-fold, 1 foot, narrow, light yellowing, good+ **$154**

Ivory rule. H. Chapin No. 58, four-fold, 1 foot, narrow, bound, tobacco yellow, good **$132**

Ivory rule. H. Chapin No. 69, four-fold, 1 foot, German silver, tobacco yellow, good **$275**

Ivory rule. H. Chapin No. 75, cased caliper, two-fold, 6", light yellowing, German silver, cased leg is stuffed w/ ivory, good **$148**

Ivory rule. Chapin-Stephens Co. No. 91, four-fold, 1 foot, tobacco yellow, fully readable, good **$165**

Ivory rule. Comparison or custom's, four-fold, 2', German silver, white, laid out in English, Russian, Rhinlan, and "Metre," fine **$495**

Ivory rule. William Slater, Bolton (designer), Aston & Mander, London (makers), cotton spinner's rule,

Ivory rule. William Slater, Bolton (designer), Aston & Mander, London (makers), cotton spinner's rule, gunther's slide, tables and instructions for cotton spinning, including revolution of spindles, counts of yarn, draught of mules, two-fold, 2', German silver, arch joint, edge marked, light yellowing, good+, $715.

gunther's slide, tables and instructions for cotton spinning, including revolution of spindles, counts of yarn, draught of mules, two-fold, 2', German silver, arch joint, edge marked, light yellowing, good+ **$715**

Ivory rule. Stanley No. 00, marked, two-fold, 6", brass fittings, light yellowing, good+ **$632**

Ivory rule. Stanley No. 38, caliper, two-fold, 6", white to light yellowing, fine **$242**

Ivory rule. Stanley No. 38, caliper, two-fold, 6", nearly snow white, fine **$275**

Ivory rule. Stanley No. 39, not marked, caliper, four-fold, 1 foot, German-silver bound, light yellowing, fine **$220**

Ivory rule. Stanley No. 39, four-fold, 1 foot, white, fine **$467**

Ivory rule. Stanley No. 40, caliper, four-fold, 1 foot, German-silver bound, light yellowing, tight joint, fine **$247**

Ivory rule. Stanley No. 40, caliper, four-fold, 1 foot, original Sweet Hart-era case, light yellowing, tight joint, fine **$495**

Ivory rule. Stanley No. 40, caliper, four-fold, 1 foot, original Sweet Hart-era case, snow white, tight joint, fine **$687**

Ivory rule. Stanley No. 40 1/2, caliper, two-fold, 6", fine **$495**

Ivory rule. Stanley No. 85, four-fold, 2', light yellowing, stress crack along edge of one leg, good+ **$121**

Ivory rule. Stanley No. 85B, marked B, brass bound, strong markings, light yellowing, fine **$1,980**

Ivory rule. Stanley No. 86, four-fold, 2', edge markings, light yellowing, good+ **$242**

Ivory rule. Stanley No. 86, four-fold, 2', strong markings, light yellowing, fine **$330**

Ivory rule. Stanley No. 86 1/2, architect's, four-fold, 2', bevel edges, minor stress lines in one leg, light yellowing, good+ **$330**

Ivory rule. Stanley No. 87, four-fold, 2', original leather case, light yellowing, joint still tight, good+ **$495**

Ivory rule. Stanley No. 87S, special bound, four-fold, 2', silver bound, slight spring to one leg, fine **$1,100**

Ivory rule. Stanley No. 88, number mark only, four-fold, 1 foot, German-silver bound, white, strong markings, stress crack on one leg, fine **$192**

Ivory rule. Stanley No. 89, four-fold, 2', German silver, tobacco yellow, light wear, no breaks or cracks, good **$440**

Ivory rule. Stanley No. 89, light yellowing, fully readable, bright, good+ **$687**

Ivory rule. Stanley No. 90, four-fold, 1 foot, narrow, light yellowing, good+ **$247**

Ivory rule. Stanley No. 92, not marked, four-fold, 1 foot, clean, white, fine **$264**

Ivory rule. Stanley No. 92 1/2, marked, four-fold, 1 foot, narrow, good+ **$550**

Ivory rule. Stanley No. 95, four-fold, 2', broad, German-silver bound, white, small dings on face, small hole in one end, fine **$3,190**

Ivory rule. Stanley No. 97, four-fold, 2', German-silver bound, arch joint, 1 5/16" wide, medium tobacco yellowing outside, light yellowing inside, some light stress cracks, good **$385**

Ivory rule. Stanley No. 97, broad, four-fold, 2', light yellowing, good **$715**

Ivory rule. A. Stanley, early, broad, four-fold, 2', light tobacco yellow, two tight cracks, some wear, good **$1,320**

Ivory rule. A. Stanley, caliper, two-fold, 6", brass trim and caliper, similar to Stanley No. 38 w/ brass trimming, only known example, tobacco yellow, fully readable but not strong, good **$770**

Ivory rule. A. Stanley, caliper, four-fold, 1 foot, German silver, light yellow, readable inside, bit faint on outside, chips along edges of caliper, good **$770**

Ivory rule. A. Stanley & Co., four-fold, 2', German-silver bound, medium yellowing, two minor stress cracks, crack in one leg, good **$825**

Ivory rule. Stanley Rule & Level, cotton staple gauge, English and metric, 3", light yellowing, ivory shows some shrinkage, fine **$1,650**

Ivory rule. E.A. Stearns & Co. No. 45, engineer's, two-fold, 2', German silver trimming and slide, light yellowing, good+ **$3,300**

Ivory rule. E.A. Stearns & Co. No 47, four-fold, 2', German silver, arch joint, extra wide, light yellowing, fine **$825**

Ivory rule. E.A. Stearns & Co. No. 47B, four-fold, 2', broad, German-silver bound, light yellowing, good+ **$605**

Ivory rule. E.A. Stearns & Co. No. 48, four-fold, 2', German silver trimmings, arch joint, edge markings, light yellowing, fine **$605**

Ivory rule. E.A. Stearns & Co. No. 50, four-fold, 2', German-silver bound, arch joint, white, engraved "W. Gay" on hinge, fine **$605**

Ivory rule. E.A. Stearns & Co. No. 50B, four-fold, 2', German-silver bound, some yellowing, strong markings, good+ **$154**

Ivory rule. E.A. Stearns & Co. No. 55 1/2, two-fold, 6", German-silver bound, cased, good+ **$385**

Ivory rule. E.A. Stearns & Co. No. 56B, four fold, 2', narrow, German-silver bound, arch joint, light yellowing, missing pins, fine **$522**

Ivory rule. E.A. Stearns & Co. No. 57, four-fold, 1 foot, narrow, white, fine **$440**

Ivory rule. E.A. Stearns & Co. No. 60, six-fold, 2', light tobacco yellowing, chip at end of one leg, good...... **$550**

Ivory rule. E.A. Stearns & Co. No. 60B, six-fold, 2', German-silver bound, arch joint, white, fine **$825**

Ivory rule. J. & G.H. Walker, New York, early, two-fold, 6", cased caliper, brass bindings and caliper, light yellowing, good+ **$880**

Ivory rule. T.B. Winter, Newcastle on Tyme, three-fold, 1 foot, narrow, arch joint, light yellowing, good+

.... **$660**

Ivory buttonhole rule. W. Harrison, Birmingham, brass tips and caliper, white, stress crack on backside at slide, fine **$220**

Ivory parallel rule. Holtzapffel & Co., German-silver fittings, 6", good+ **$220**

Lady's leg caliper. Garter, 9", good+ **$203**

Lady's leg caliper. P. Lowentraut, Newark, N.J., 2 1/2", good+ **$77**

Lady's leg caliper. Skinny legs, 8 1/2", fine **$99**

Layout tool. Bostock & Pancoast, Philadelphia, patented, Aug. 6, 1867, and May 23, 1871, adjusts for angle and width between rule and square face, good **$121**

Ledger rule. Wyckoff, combination rule, patented, Aug. 15, 1876, and July 31, 1877, 12", metal paint about 85%, good **$60**

Log caliper. F.M. Greenleaf, Belmont, Mass., cordwood calipers, "G" cast into brass jaws supports, scales bright and readable, marked wheel by C.W. Grover, Caratunk, Maine, good+ **$1,705**

Log caliper. William Greenleaf, Littleton, N.H., unmarked Grover wheel, scales stamped, fully readable, good+ **$990**

Log cane. Stanley No. 48 1/2, marked Stanley, New Britain logo and number, hickory, brass end caps, much original finish, fine **$220**

Log cane. Stanley Tool & Level Co. No. 48 1/2, marked, hickory, brass cap and tip, fully readable, fine......... **$148**

Log rule. V. Fabian's son, Milo Junction, Maine, scales on all four sides, laid out in Maine log or Holland scale, paper label fully readable w/ only minor edge wear, yellow finish 95%, good+... **$143**

Log scale. Cleveland Rule Co. No. 15D, Doyle scale, fully readable and clear, fine..**$71**

Log stick. Lufkin Rule Co. No. 22, Saginaw, Mich., Scribner's decimal C scale, brass head, laminated handle, 5', fine **$50**

Machinist's square. Starrett No. 20, 18", precision steel, good+..**$60**

Machinist's square. Starrett No. 20, 24", precision steel, wood stand, good+ **$121**

Machinist's square. Starrett No. 20, 36", precision steel, wood stand, good+ **$121**

Marking gauge. Beam locks in place w/ a chuck similar to hand drill, rosewood head, plated beam about 95%, good+..**$192**

Marking gauge. Blaisdell patent, June 23, 1868, rosewood, brass, lever-action adjustment rotates pawls to work curves, chip on edge of head, one screw not brass, good **$192**

Marking gauge. Extra-long brass head, square steel rod, good+..**$55**

Marking gauge. Kinney patent, shown in 1885 Sandusky Tool Co. catalog, notched rotating head, couple of chips on wheel, good................................. **$577**

Marking gauge. Marples, ebony, heavy brass head, weak mark, good...**$77**

Marking gauge. Schol patent, rosewood, four stems, good **$110**

Marking gauge. Welsh patent, two sliding sections, brass fittings, trace of original finish, good+ **$50**

Marking gauges. Welsh patent, Feb. 3, 1891, patent date fully readable, Winslow adjustable face patent, Oct. 23, 1900, two sliding sections, brass fittings, rosewood beam, fine..**$165**

Mortise gauge. C. Sholl patent, March 6, 1864, rosewood, four stems, brass wear plates and slide, fine, $121.

Micrometers. Starrett No. 230 1", No. 226 in five sizes from 1" to 5", original wood case, fine...................... **$253**

Mortise gauge. E.W. Carpenter, Lancaster, rosewood, boxwood slide and screw, good+............................... **$187**

Mortise gauge. Phillips patent, two brass heads, ebony beam, double brass slides on both sides of beam for two sets of adjustable points, English take on American patent, good... **$160**

Mortise gauge. C. Sholl patent, March 6, 1864, rosewood, three stems, round disks for wear plates in head, brass slide adjuster in beam, good+ **$132**

Mortise gauge. C. Sholl patent, March 6, 1864, rosewood, four stems, brass wear plates and slide, fine **$121**

Mortise gauge. C. Sholl patent, March 6, 1864, rosewood, four stems, brass screw and slide, good+ **$154**

Mortise gauge. Stanley No. 77, marked, metric, rosewood, brass fittings, new, fine............................ **$605**

Mortise gauge. Stanley No. 90, eagle trademark, Williams patent, rosewood head, steel wear plate, brass beam, chip off head, good **$165**

Outside calipers. Bronze, 13 1/2", quarter-arc locking adjustment, fine.. **$82**

Outside calipers. Not marked, probably manufactured, brass, steel legs, joint, and arch, 38", fine **$440**

Panel gauge. Stanley No. 84, marked, handled, locking screw for cutter on end of beam, fine **$467**

Panel gauge. Stanley No. 85, marked, good+.......... **$165**

Pitch gauge. Stanley No. 5, for wooden level, plating 97%, fine.. **$209**

Proof rule. Loftus, London, slide, boxwood, tables on both sides, calculates proof and shillings per quart, 11", good+...**$27**

Protractor squares. Starrett, not marked, pair, different designs, one vial missing, japanning 65%, good **$137**

Ring-sizing rule. Rabone, four sides, scales on each face, fine **$88**

Rule. Early, handwrought iron, 12 5/8", no numbers, semicircular decoration, good **$55**

Rule. Farrand No. 100, rapid rule, instructions, original green box, plating 100%, fine.......................................**$88**

Rule. Lufkin No. 2071, advertising for Lufkin rules on one side, three-fold, 1 foot w/ level, weak printing, good **$165**

Rule. Stanley special No. 41, 48", maple, brass tips, hang hole, good+ **$88**

Rule. A. Stanley & Co. No. 66, boxwood, four-fold, 3', stain at joint, traces of finish, good **$1,045**

Rule attachment. J. McManus, San Francisco, patented, Feb. 27, 1894, hinged portion flips up 90 degrees and locks device in place, device can be used as a stop once

Rule attachment. J. McManus, San Francisco, patented, Feb. 27, 1894, hinged portion flips up 90 degrees and locks device in place, device can be used as a stop once locked, two examples on a Stanley No. 68, one w/ brass finish and marked, the other plated and unmarked, fine, $264.

locked, two examples on a Stanley No. 68, one w/ brass finish and marked, the other plated and unmarked, fine
....**$264**

Rule-making stamps. Smallwood factory, for rope gauges and 12" rules, six unfinished rules, includes stamp probably for box labels, good+......................**$176**

Rule-making tool. Smallwood Factory, Birmingham, England, stamp for boxwood rules, marks one leg of a four-fold 2-foot rule, good+ **$165**

Rule manufacturing collection. From Smallwood factory, eight bars for stamping rules, eight blocks for printing catalogs, eight rules in progress, nine rule maker's hand stamps, early pages from Smallwood catalog, good and better.. **$264**

Ruling device. I.C. Walk, Chambersburg, Pa., patented, March 4, 1911, purpose unknown, aluminum frame, two wood inserts, two steel rods run down center w/ space on both sides, good+ **$27**

Screen-sizing slip rule. Porter Screen Manufacturing Co., made by Kerby & Brothers, New York, two-fold, slides to 50", fine **$27**

Ship carpenter's bevel. Stanley No. 42 1/2, c. 1885, not marked, rosewood, brass blade, friction joint, good+ **$302**

Ship carpenter's bevel. Stanley No. 42 1/2, marked Stanley on brass blade, rosewood, fine **$467**

Sliding T bevel. Stanley, patented, Sept. 4, 1887, improved, walnut infill, 10", good **$412**

Slitting gauge. Grisard, Paris, slitting leg hinged and swings on semicircular locking arc, adjustable divider legs w/ quarter-circle locking arc, good+ **$209**

Slitting gauge. A.W. Mack, Brooklyn Township, Pa.,
 marked, tiger maple, wedges locks on cutter and beam,
 fine **$176**
Slitting gauge. Thomas Rice patent, Sept. 8, 1873,
 rosewood and brass, round cutter rotates as cut is made,
 good+..**$632**

*Slitting gauge. Thomas Rice patent, Sept. 8, 1873, rosewood
and brass, round cutter rotates as cut is made, good+, $632.*

Storekeeper's caliper. Lufkin Rule Co., "Coopers Kenosha-Klosed-Krotch Union Suits", for sizing "Three Season Wear" underwear, signed in pencil by Banford Cooper, fine **$137**

Square. Ivory, brass-pinned mortise and tenon joint, blade 5", good+ **$176**

Square. A. McKenzie patent, April 21, 1857, brass handle, steel blade, swing-out bevel w/ direct reading scale for polygons, blade 9", fine **$220**

Square. A. McKenzie patent, April 21, 1857, brass handle, steel blade, swing-out bevel w/ direct reading scale for polygons, blade 9", fine, $220.

Square. Patented, Nov. 11, 1884, patent-date mark only, folding handle can be set from 0 to 180 degrees, stop sets 90 degrees, other angles read from graduated scale around handle, beam graduated in inches, good+.....**$66**

Square. "Patent Applied For", name mark not readable, rosewood, brass-bound handle, square blade on one edge, bevel on other, good..**$198**

Tape rule. Stanley Four Square No. 1166, advertising, Cincinnati Producers, fine+.......................................**$154**

Tape rule. Stanley Four Square No. 1166, advertising, Cincinnati Producers, fine+, $154.

Trammels. Heavy cast brass, star on one side, slash on other, steel points, 9", fine... **$330**

Trammels. Brass, steel tips, brass-bound beam 23", points 8", probably manufactured, good+.............................**$55**

Trammels. Brass, almost 11" tall, harplike motif on each body, fine... **$264**

Trammels. Heavy brass, two inside-type heads, one nonmatching point, 11 1/2", good+ **$105**

Trammels. Heavy cast brass, star on one side, slash on other, steel points, 9", fine, $330.

Trammels. Heavy cast bronze, spring-loaded fine adjustment, steel points, 4 1/2", good+ **$82**

Trammels. A.J. Wilkinson, Boston, brass, heart-shaped open work, steel points, 5", good+ **$105**

Traveler. A. Czirr, 1890, heavy iron handle w/ looped end, graduated to 20", teardrop pointer indicates zero mark, good+ **$165**

Traveler. A. Czirr, 1890, heavy iron handle w/ looped end, graduated to 20", teardrop pointer indicates zero mark, good+, $165.

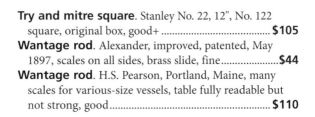

Traveler. Wood spoke wheel, red paint, yellow and black pinstriping, turned wood handle, 23", good+, $308.

Try and mitre square. Stanley No. 22, 12", No. 122 square, original box, good+ **$105**

Wantage rod. Alexander, improved, patented, May 1897, scales on all sides, brass slide, fine.....................**$44**

Wantage rod. H.S. Pearson, Portland, Maine, many scales for various-size vessels, table fully readable but not strong, good..**$110**

Saws

Saws, with their distinctive serrated teeth, probably have their origins in specialized stone tools of Neolithic times. The ancient Greeks are credited with the development of hand-hammered iron saw blades, but the ancient Egyptians also made use of this tool.

The earliest saw blades were fitted in a wooden framework for support, and saws of this style are still used today. By the late 17th century, wider blades of hardened steel could be operated using only a cutout handle at one end. The saw became ever more refined during the 18th and 19th centuries, and blades of all shapes and sizes were available as the Industrial Revolution progressed. Today's basic handsaw has not changed greatly from its 18th century ancestors.

Backsaw. Disston, steel back runs full length of blade and is removable for making through cuts, apple-wood handle, previously William Zearfoss collection, fine, $3,630.

Backsaw. "Di… Co.", brass back, split nuts, early style handle, blade 19", good...**$71**

Backsaw. Disston, steel back runs full length of blade and is removable for making through cuts, apple-wood handle, previously William Zearfoss collection, fine **$3,630**

Backsaw. Henry Disston & Son, brass back, blade etching fully readable, stamped brass back, bottom tang has some damage, good **$192**

Backsaw. Patent 119403, brass backed, unusual handle, blade 8", good...**$82**

Backsaw. N.H. Theding, Dubuque, Iowa, 14", split nuts, some of top tang on handle lost, good...................... **$192**

Butcher's saw. Richardson No. 7, knife blade on one side, saw on other, weak mark, good+.........................**$71**

Cabinetmaker's framed veneer saw. Mortise and tenon joints, beaded frame, handles at each corner, blade 30", fine.. **$385**

Dovetail saw. Independence Tool, original Pete Taran production, maple handle, brass back, fine **$165**

Frame saw. 18th century, hornlike handle on one end of blade, wood rod and nut tensioner, carved frame and stretcher, blade 9", good+ **$165**

Frame saw. Early, mortise and tenon construction, possibly hickory, blade 29", good **$22**

Combination handsaw. Disston No. 43, brass level, rule, scratch awl, square, more, etching fully readable, good+, $1,210.

Framed pit saw. Wood frame, handles top and bottom, tensioned iron rod on one side, more than 5' tall, good+, $330.

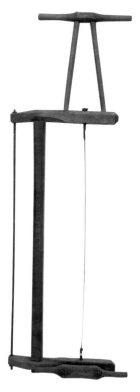

*Framed pit saw. Wood box
frame, handles top and bottom,
tensioned w/ iron yoke, 6' tall, 3'
wide, some worm, good, $907.*

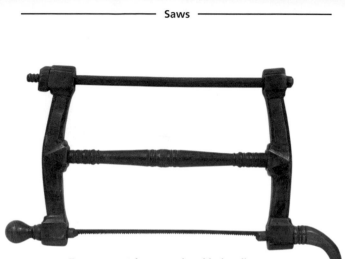

Frame saw. 18th century, hornlike handle on one end of blade, wood rod and nut tensioner, carved frame and stretcher, blade 9", good+, $165.

Frame saw. Mortise and tenon construction, ram's horn nut tension bolt, blade 20", good+ **$77**

Framed bow saw. Double handle, blade 24", hand-cut bolts, good+ **$115**

Fretsaw. Maple, throat depth 12", blade 4", fine.......**$110**

Fretsaw. Dark rosewood, 12", fine **$165**

Fretsaw. Light rosewood, good....................................**$110**

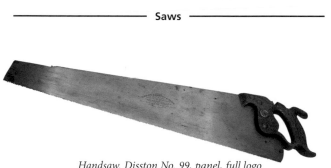

*Handsaw. Disston No. 99, panel, full logo
and tote, blade 22", 8 TPI, fine, $82.*

Fretsaw. Rosewood, adjustable handle, blade 4", good
....**$71**

Fretsaw. Rosewood or mahogany, throat depth 18", blade
4 1/2", good+ **$77**

Handsaw. Atkins Perfection No. 53 demonstration saw,
for teaching saw filing, edge sometimes incorrectly
filed in inches, chip off top tang on handle, blade fully
readable, good+... **$330**

Handsaw. Disston & Morss No. 43, level, awl, square,
rule, and saw all in one, blade clean, replacement top
tang on handle, good...**$192**

Handsaw. Woodrough & McParlin, Cincinnati, Ohio,
carved panther head on handle, traces of round patent-
date ink stamp, blade barely readable, repaired top tang,
good **$715**

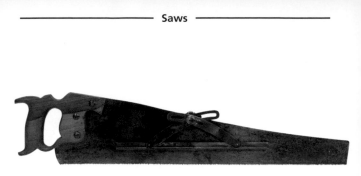

Handsaw. Kramer No. 14, adjustable stop can be set for various angles and depths, 10 PTI, good, $357.

Japanese ripsaw. Edge 21", 13" deep, replaced handle, good **$198**

Japanese saw. For ripping boards from a log, smaller than typical, possibly for veneer sawing, good+ **$99**

Japanese saw. Pull type, good+ **$66**

Pruning saw. W. Brand, cast steel, carved handle, brass ferrule, 33", good.. **$341**

Saw set. Lasso, universal, various anvils and plungers, original wood box, good+ **$110**

Saw set. Lever type, brass head, adjustable, ebonized handles, good+ **$132**

Saw set. Preston, not marked, hammer set, bench type, good **$38**

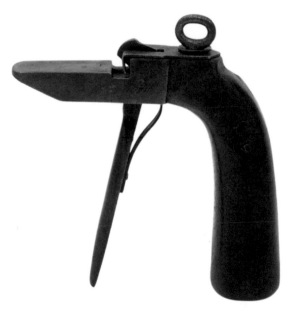

Saw set. Remington Chase patent, Feb. 15, 1866, pistol grip, good+, $192.

Saw set. Remington Chase patent, Feb. 15, 1866, pistol grip, good+ **$192**

Scroll saw. American Scroll Saw, Delta Specialty Co., Milwaukee, Wis., hand crank or run w/ round belt, works smoothly, paint about 90%, fine........................**$71**

Spruce-gum saw. For gathering spruce gum in Maine forest, handwrought, two blades, one coarse for limbs and one fine for gum balls, handle shortened for display, blade 24", good+ **$77**

Turning saw. Burl and tiger maple, highly figured, 18", modern, fine...**$231**

Turning saw. Rosewood handles, ivory tensioner, blade 10", good+..**$137**

Turning saw. Wrought-iron frame, one handle has hang hole as part of design, good+ **$247**

Turning saw. Wrought-iron frame, one handle has hang hole as part of design, good+, $247.

Turning saw. Possibly mahogany, small size, ivory
tensioner, good+ **$110**
Veneer saw. Early, possibly walnut, ivory tensioner,
scroll work w/ decoration, good **$330**

*Turning saw. Possibly mahogany, small
size, ivory tensioner, good+, $110.*

Veneer saw. Lion trademark, blade 22", good+ **$192**
Veneer saw. Oriental, rosewood, bamboo, blade 18",
  good+..**$38**

*Veneer saw. Early, possibly walnut, ivory
tensioner, scroll work w/ decoration, good, $330.*

Scientific
Instruments

Some tools fall into a technical classification because they are used for more precise measurement than needed in rough carpentry work and common household use. And as society has become increasingly mechanized and complex, tools have become correspondingly more sophisticated. With modern developments came the need for extremely exacting tolerances. Thus, for example, the need was born for surveying equipment that could accurately measure the precise distances and angles needed to erect skyscrapers, and for engineering rules that enabled drafters to create airplane designs. Of course, now we have far surpassed these early precision tools with computerized drafting and design, GPS to aid navigation and surveying, etc. But the tools listed in this section were those that helped launch the modern industrial and technical era.

Cooper's compass. Elm, double action, 10", iron points, some pitting, fine **$165**

Drafting instrument. K&E, protractor, 180-degree swing, fitted case, fine **$71**

Engineer's transit. K&E No. 5060A, serial No. 29097, scope 11", silvered vertical circle 5", compass needle 5", black finish about 80%, repaired original box, good **$247**

Engineer's transit and tripod. C.L. Berger & Sons, serial No. 15785, brass finish, scope 11 1/4", compass needle 4 1/4", vertical arch 5", sunshade missing, original box, labels inside and out, good.................. **$302**

Mining instrument. Dip needle, brass case w/ double covers, locking pin and chain, fine..............................**$60**

Navigational instrument. J.W. Strange, Bangor, Maine, patented, June 13, 1876, T square w/ plated rotating dial for setting compass course, few spots on brass, good+ **$82**

Scientific instrument. Franz Schmidt & Haensch Berlin L. No. 22, possibly refraction measuring device, brass and iron base, fine **$247**

Sighting instrument. W.N. Matthews Corp., hand level, vial sits on top at 45-degree angle and is read through tube, leather case, fine...**$82**

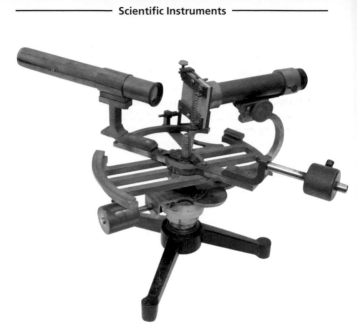

*Scientific instrument. Franz Schmidt & Haensch
Berlin L. No. 22, possibly refraction measuring
device, brass and iron base, fine, $247.*

Sighting level. Starrett patent, level w/ sighting tube and transit, wood case holds instrument and tripod, japanning 90%, good..**$93**

Surveyor's chain. 100', brass handles and tags, no rust, good+..**$121**

Surveyor's chain. Chesterman, marked "1Chain" on end of handles, brass tags and handles, probably galvanized, good+..**$143**

Surveyor's chain. K&E No. 12, tested, 100', welded links, brass handles and tags, good+..........................**$110**

Surveyor's chain. T.F. Randolph, Cincinnati, Ohio, brass handles, several repaired links, good **$137**

Surveyor's chain and pins. K&E No. 12, steel, 100', brass handles and tags, eight station pins, good and better..**$165**

Surveying instrument. American Waywise, early 19th or possibly 18th century, two brass dials located behind hinge cover record distance as wheel rotates, handmade screws, hand-stamped brass, good+ **$1,760**

Surveying instrument. B. Becmdeper No. 89, circumferenter, brass table 10" in diameter, four brass sighting vanes, level and compass dial, needle 4 3/8", brass cover, wood case, good+ **$550**

*Surveying instrument. American
Waywise, early 19th or possibly
18th century, two brass dials located
behind hinge cover record distance
as wheel rotates, handmade screws,
hand-stamped brass, good+, $1,760.*

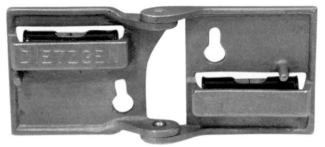

Surveying instrument. Dietzen, rod level, two vials can lie flat or be folded at 90 degrees, two posts on body can be attached to rod w/ rubber bands or screw attached w/ two keyhole holes, fine, $110.

Surveying instrument. C.L. Berger & Sons, Boston, 9403, engineer's transit, optional jointed magnifying glass attached to frame, side-mounted focus, silvered dial 4", needle 3 1/2", scope 9 1/2", silvered vertical circle 5", two level vials, one on table, one on frame, original box, tripod, good **$385**

Surveying instrument. C.L. Berger & Sons, Boston, 29213, engineer's transit, side-mounted focus, silvered dial 4", needle 3 1/2", scope 11", silvered vertical circle 5", two level vials, black finish nearly perfect, original box, tripod, fine... **$440**

Surveying instrument. E. & G.W. Blunt, New York, 261, c. 1830s, vernier compass, adjusting knob on underside, scale above, silvered dial 6", needle 5 3/4", sighting vanes 6", two leveling vials, fine **$1,925**

Surveying instrument. Buff & Buff Manufacturing Co., patented, July 11, 1916, transit, dial 3 1/2", needle 3", scope 10", full vertical and horizontal circles, finish 92%, original case, good+ **$385**

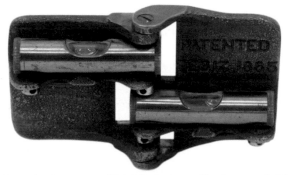

Surveying instrument. W. & L.E. Gurley, rod level, patented, Feb. 17, 1885, two vials can lie flat or be folded at 90 degrees, two hooks on body for attaching to rod w/ rubber bands, fine, $60.

Surveying instrument. Cross, brass, two sets of sights at 90 degrees, socket for staff mount, good+ **$121**

Surveying instrument. W.C. Davis, New York, vernier compass, adjusting dial to side of table, dial 5 1/2", needle 4 3/4", vanes 6 1/2", two level vials, counter w/ dial, original box marked "S. Thaxter & Son", label in top, fine.. **$1,650**

Surveying instrument. Dietzen, rod level, two vials can lie flat or be folded at 90 degrees, two posts on body can be attached to rod w/ rubber bands or screw attached w/ two keyhole holes, fine.. **$110**

Surveying instrument. W. & L.E. Gurley, rod level, patented, Feb. 17, 1885, two vials can lie flat or be folded at 90 degrees, two hooks on body for attaching to rod w/ rubber bands, fine **$60**

Surveying instrument. W. & L.E. Gurley, Troy, N.Y., cruiser's compass, marked "Forrest Service" on underside, silvered dial 4", needle 3 1/2", double leveling vials, post on base for staff, compass needle locks from underside, some original finish, leather case, part of strap missing, good+ **$165**

Surveying instrument. W. & L.E. Gurley, Troy, N.Y., engineer's transit, A frame, side-mounted focus, silvered dial 6", needle 5 1/2", scope 11 1/2", vertical circle 4 1/2", two level vials, one on table, one on frame, sun shade, tripod, good+ **$495**

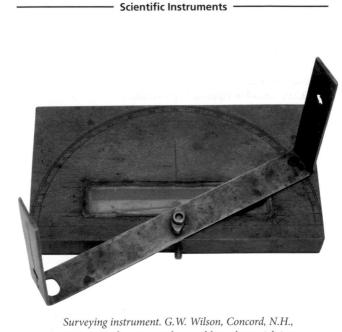

*Surveying instrument. G.W. Wilson, Concord, N.H.,
semicircumfermeter, early, wood base, brass sighting
vane and compass needle, hand stamped, Wilson's
business card in wood case w/ instrument, some repair
work on instrument likely done by Wilson, good+, $550.*

Surveying instrument. W. & L.E. Gurley, Troy, N.Y., 16111, hellgate transit, c. 1920, brass finish, side-mounted focus, silvered dial 3 1/2" and marked "Case School of Applied Engineering. Dept. of Civil Engineering. No. 38.", needle 3", scope 8 1/2", vertical circle 4 1/2", two level vials, sunshade, box, good+ **$605**

Surveying instrument. W. & L.E. Gurley, Troy, N.Y., light mountain transit, c. 1890, modified A frame, side-mounted focus, dial 4 1/2", needle 4", scope 8 1/2", vertical half arc 5", two level vials, sun shade, tripod, box w/ leather case, leather box cover worn, good+ **$825**

Surveying instrument. W. & L.E. Gurley, pocket compass, fold-up sights, locking dial, brass belt ring, black finish 93%, good+..**$27**

Surveying instrument. W. & L.E. Gurley, Troy, N.Y., reconnaissance transit, c. 1890, modified A frame, side-mounted focus, silvered dial 4", needle 3 1/2", scope 9", vertical circle 3 1/2", two level vials, sun shade, tripod w/ two stiff legs and one adjustable, box, paper label, good+.. **$1,320**

Surveying instrument. W. & L.E. Gurley, Troy, N.Y., surveyor's transit, c. 1875, A frame, side-mounted focus, silvered dial 5 1/2" and marked "F.W. Lincoln Jr. & Co. Agents. Boston Mass.", needle 5", scope 11", vertical

circle 4 1/2", two level vials, one on frame, box, good+
.... **$770**

Surveying instrument. W. & L.E. Gurley, Troy, N.Y.,
16111, surveyor's transit, c. 1900, side-mounted focus,
silvered dial 5 1/2", needle 5", scope 11", vertical circle

Vernier compass. Edmund Draper, Philadelphia,
dial 6 1/2", needle 5 1/2", vanes 7 1/4", cross vials for
level and plumb, cover, wood case, good+, $1,265.

4 1/2", two level vials, sun shade, tripod, brass accents, japanning 90%, box, good+...**$330**

Surveying instrument. W. & L.E. Gurley, vernier compass, scale under glass, knob below plate, dial 5 1/2", needle 5", vanes 7 1/2", two vials, counter, socket and ball for Jacob's staff, original box, label in top, complete strap, fine... **$1,430**

Vernier compass. T. Mason, Essex Bridge,
Dublin, brass, 19" overall, dial 6 3⁄8", needle
5 1⁄4", vanes 8 1⁄2", dial cover, good+, $1,430.

Surveying instrument. Jacob's staff, socket and ball, iron point, fine **$605**

Surveying instrument. A. Meneely Sons, West Troy, N.Y., vernier compass, adjuster at side of table, two level vials, one dry, dial 6 1/2", needle 6", vanes 7 1/2", box, key, good+ **$2,145**

Surveying instrument. G.W. Wilson, Concord, N.H., semicircumfermeter, early, wood base, brass sighting vane and compass needle, hand stamped, Wilson's business card in wood case w/ instrument, some repair work on instrument likely done by Wilson, good+ **$550**

Vernier compass. Edmund Draper, Philadelphia, dial 6 1/2", needle 5 1/2", vanes 7 1/4", cross vials for level and plumb, cover, wood case, good+ **$1,265**

Vernier compass. T. Mason, Essex Bridge, Dublin, brass, 19" overall, dial 6 3/8", needle 5 1/4", vanes 8 1/2", dial cover, good+ **$1,430**

Special Use & Miscellaneous Tools

This section covers a wide variety of tools that don't fit neatly into broad categories included earlier. Often these are tools of a very specialized nature used by specific craftsmen or in certain trades. You may see tools listed here that are not easily recognized by the non-specialist collector. With luck you may find out what that mysterious "what's-it" is that you've found during your collecting forays.

Apple parer. Wood, peg-type gear, hand held, good+ **$33**

Apple peeler. Reading Hardware Co., numerous patents starting in 1872, cast iron, good+............................ **$110**

Beader. Glock & Tallmadge, Columbus, Ohio, Windsor patent, March 10 and June 2, 1885, ebonized, good+ **$148**

Beader. Windsor, type 1, walnut, much original finish, fine, $440.

Beader. Stanley No. 69, single hand, plating 60%, good **$220**

Beader. Stanley No. 69, c. 1915, single hand, one cutter, plating 97%, fine **$275**

Beader. Windsor, patented, March 10, 1885, and June 2, 1885, ebonized hardwood handle, brass face, good **$137**

Beader. Windsor, patented, Sept. 15, 1885, type 2, slotted body, rosewood T handles, three double-ended cutters, plating 50%, good **$440**

Beader. Windsor, type 1, walnut, much original finish, fine **$440**

Beam scale. Sargent No. 200, clear mark, original weight, good+ **$55**

Bear trap. Mounted on board for display, 36", jaws 9", temper pulled from springs, good **$148**

Bevel square. L.D. Howard patent, Nov. 5, 1867, 7 1/2", "W.H. Stebbins" owner mark, brass handle w/ level, fancy casting, good+ **$176**

Blacksmith's forge bellows. Possibly New Hampshire, more than 6' long, air spout and hardware present, no signs of soot or coke dust, old red paint nearly perfect, all leather intact, fine **$687**

Blind nailing tool. Stanley No. 96, marked Stanley and w/ patent date, storage stain on one side, good+ **$198**

Blacksmith's forge bellows. Possibly New Hampshire, more than 6' long, air spout and hardware present, no signs of soot or coke dust, old red paint nearly perfect, all leather intact, fine, $687.

Board cane. Belcher Brothers, New York, brass tips, hickory, fully readable, good+ **$165**
Board cane. Kerby & Davidson, New York, brass tips, maple, fully readable, good+ **$280**
Board cane. J. Pearce, Albany, brass tips, fully readable, good **$275**

Board cane. L. Ward, Newark, N.J., brass tips, hickory, fully readable, good+..**$495**

Bookbinder's creasers. Set of 19, "LEM" engraved on several, most handles match, larger size, good..........**$77**

Brad awls. Stanley No. 3, set of seven in original box, handled, box has tear on one corner, fine................**$143**

Bridge builder's plumb bob. Cast iron, brass cap, 13 pounds, 13", good+..**$286**

Bridge builder's plumb bob. Steel top section and tip, 9", good+ **$132**

Buggy wrench. Thumbscrew adjusts to size of nut, good **$687**

Clamps. Stanley Rule & Level Co., wood, 18", some thread damage, good..**$82**

Clockmaker's bench vise. Marked "No. 1", early, handwrought, short post, for use at a low bench, bench bracket, 27", jaws 4", complete, good..........................**$71**

Combination anvil and vise. C. Parker No. 19, Meriden, Conn., bench type, good..............................**$55**

Combination anvil and vise. C. Parker No. 21, Meriden, Conn., bench type w/ washer, plate and nut, jaws 3 1/4", good..**$38**

Combination anvil and vise. I. Peter, Lenz, c. 1800, jaw 2 3/8", bench thumbscrew, good+......................**$148**

Chopper. Wood handle in shape of a horse, old green paint, good+, $165.

Combination tool. Cie des Clefs Universelles Port a Outils Multiples, bench vise, adze, saw, wrench, ax, brass and iron, original box, label glued to top, good+, $1,815.

*Combination framing tool.
Standard Framer Co., patented,
June 1, 1920, square, bevel, level,
japanning 95%, fine, $302.*

Combination tool. Stanley No. 1 Odd Jobs, no-patent-date type, complete, No. 27 Sweet Hart folding rule, plating 85% and dull, good **$132**

Conestoga wagon jack. Early, burl body, handmade, good **$110**

Conestoga wagon jack. "GxB 1825," date on post, handmade, much file decoration, good **$105**

Conestoga wagon jack. "G+B 1827," date on post, handmade, much file decoration, good **$225**

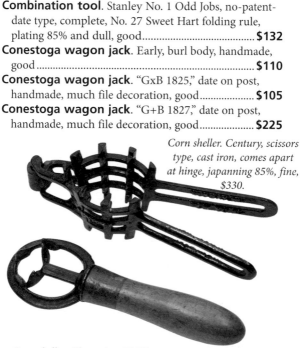

Corn sheller. Century, scissors type, cast iron, comes apart at hinge, japanning 85%, fine, $330.

Corn sheller. Champion, T. Weaver patent, April 12, 1870, Harrisburg, Pa., wood handle, outside loop w/spring-loaded inside jaw adjusts to ear size, faint paper label, fine, $1,100.

Cooper's chime maul. For knocking on chime hoops, iron, heavy, good+ **$16**

Cooper's howel and croze. Matched pair, good+ **$137**

Corn sheller. F&F Co., Springfield, Ohio, patented, July 6, 1869, bird, spring-loaded jaws encased in circular cast-iron head, wood handle pivots for left- or right-handed use, japanning 96%, fine **$302**

Corn sheller. Century, scissors type, cast iron, comes apart at hinge, japanning 85%, fine **$330**

Crown molders. Iohn Fisher, matched pair, Pennsylvania Dutch influence, larger crown marked three times w/ two different Fisher stamps, both marked "HKL", wide flat chamfers, offset totes w/ long tails, applied fences, good+ **$2,640**

Foundry tools. About 30 tools, steel shaping tools, wooden sand rammer, stand-up rammer in two pieces, screws together w/ brass ferrule, original tradesman's box w/ lift-out tray, good and better **$143**

Fruit devil. Loosens fruit from barrel, double wings, spiral tip, good **$165**

Furniture jack. Brady Manufacturing Co., Mount Joy, Pa., patented, July 6, 1869, hand crank operates rack-and-pinion mechanism, good **$88**

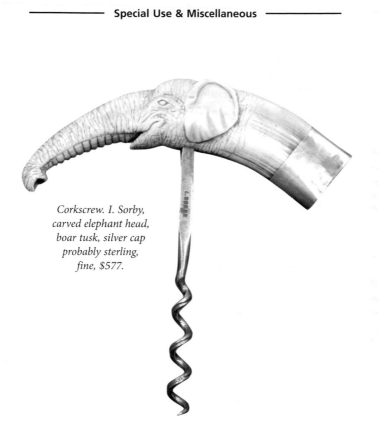

Corkscrew. I. Sorby, carved elephant head, boar tusk, silver cap probably sterling, fine, $577.

Grain balance scale. Brass, brass pail, slide weight reads weight per bushel based on full measure of grain, good+ **$137**

Grease or tallow box. Possibly walnut, heart shaped, swing lid, good+..**$66**

Hand beader. Stanley No. 66, universal, eight cutters, two fences, original box worn, label 70%, plating 98%, good+..**$132**

Hand beader. Stanley No. 69, seven cutters, plating 55%, good **$330**

Hand beader. Windsor, type 1, wood, good............**$176**

Hand vise. Possibly 18th century,
handwrought, engraved, decorated, good, $286.

Hand vise. Possibly 18th century, handwrought, engraved, decorated, good...**$286**

Hanging tongs. Highly decorated, iron arms file and stamp decorated, brass scissor-action top end pulls tips together and holds load, brass decorated, good **$126**

Horse measure. Owner made, folds, opens to measure up to 18 hands, removable caliper jaw w/ level, good **$220**

Ice-harvesting tongs. Handwrought including chain that joins two tongs at top, 35", good...........................**$50**

Letter press. L. Bailey, 15" by 22", finish 95%, good+, $330.

Letter press. L. Bailey, 15" by 22", finish 95%, good+ **$330**

Lumber cane. A. Stanley & Co., New Britain, hickory, brass cap and tip, good+ **$3,300**

Miner's sticking tommy. Handwrought, open work, spring candle clip, ornate, fine **$467**

Mitre box. Standard, patented, Aug. 20, 1889, open work table w/ floral designs, back decorated w/ cast-in designs in Eastlake style, saw, chips on saw bar, good **$176**

Mitre jack. Flat, man trudging home in sunshine carved on one side, dovetailed, 20", good **$38**

Lumber cane. A. Stanley & Co., New Britain, hickory, brass cap and tip, good+, $3,300.

Mitre jack. Maple, 8", wood screw, good......................**$38**
Odd jobs. Stanley, original rule w/ proper point, level, original scribe, plating 90%, good.............................**$187**
Odd jobs. Stanley No. 1, rule 12", original long green box w/ edge wear, fine..**$495**
Oiler. Long nose, pumper type, 20", brass fill cap, good **$66**
Paint grinder. O.C. Harris, Waterville, N.Y., repatented, August 1848, hopper at top, crank handle rotates grinder, three legs can be bolted down, foot on one leg repaired, good **$50**

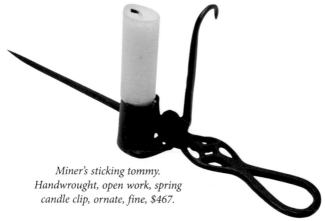

Miner's sticking tommy. Handwrought, open work, spring candle clip, ornate, fine, $467.

Paper hanger's plumb bob. Acorn finial, steel point, 2 1/4", fine..**$143**

Piano tuner's kit. Fancy wood case w/ top-of-the-line tools, six center drawers hold selection of tools and supplies, top and bottom lids open for access to fitted tool compartments, some tool clips missing, good+
....**$247**

Pipe wrench. Stanley, Sweet Hart, 10", fine.................**$93**

Pipe wrench. Stanley No. 80B, beryllium, 18", new but most of paint in one of handle recesses lost, rest of finish 98%, fine...**$247**

Piano tuner's kit. Fancy wood case w/ top-of-the-line tools, six center drawers hold selection of tools and supplies, top and bottom lids open for access to fitted tool compartments, some tool clips missing, good+, $247.

Plane maker's floats and saw. G. Inglis, set of seven, different cuts and shapes, good+ **$605**

Plumb bob. Possibly 18th century, small iron tip, 4 1/2", good **$154**

Plumb bob. Brass, bulbous, steel tip, 9", good+ **$385**

Plumb bob. Brass, even tapered design, steel tip, 4 1/2", good+ **$99**

Plane maker's floats and saw. G. Inglis, set of seven, different cuts and shapes, good+, $605.

Plumb bob. Brass, lead core, steel center and point, 5", fitted wood case w/ screw-on cap probably original, good+ **$93**

Plumb bob. Cast brass, steel tip, cylinder 2 1/2", 6", good+ **$154**

Plumb bob. Cast brass, steel tip, round, diameter about 3", hollow, possibly meant to be filled w/ lead, good+ **$170**

Plumb bob. Cast brass, two pieces w/ large ornate thread cap, base end has steel tip and threads into cap, 3 3/4", good+ **$121**

Plumb bob. Cast iron, ring string holder, ornate casting, 3 1/4", good **$105**

Plumb bob. Copper, steel point, 6", diameter 1 5/8", good **$170**

Plumb bob. Copper Age, 1 1/2", good **$88**

Plumb bob. H.M. Curry patent, June 10, 1902, pear shaped, two parts w/ hollow center, spring-loaded mechanism controls string, cap and point screw hold halves together, good+ **$660**

Plumb bob. Decorative, flowers and animals cast around sides, cast brass, steel tip, 9", fine **$137**

Plumb bob. Egg shaped, brass, extra long steel tip, 7", minor pitting on tip, good **$148**

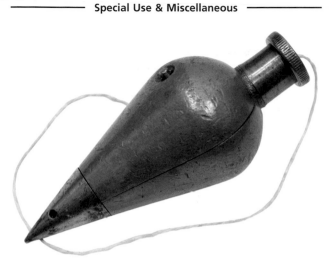

Plumb bob. H.M. Curry patent, June 10, 1902, pear shaped, two parts w/ hollow center, spring-loaded mechanism controls string, cap and point screw hold halves together, good+, $660.

Plumb bob. Gunmetal, steel point, 5 1/2", good+
.... **$121**
Plumb bob. Ivory, brass cap and point holder, steel point, fine **$275**
Plumb bob. Ivory, reel w/ brass center rod, 2 1/2" long, diameter about 1/2", turned finials, light yellowing, good+.. **$115**

Plumb bob. K&E, mechanical, internal reel rolls up line, good **$181**

Plumb bob. Keen Kutter, plating 92% and bright, shrinkage crack on cap wound w/ thread long ago, original wood case w/ screw cap, good+ **$71**

Plumb bob. Needle, cast brass, steel tip, 8", diameter 1 3/8" at widest point, good+ **$181**

Plumb bob. S in a shield, brass, steel tip, 4", fine **$50**

Plumb bob. Turnip, brass, steel tip, 7", good+ **$176**

Plumb bob. Turnip, brass, steep tip, 7 1/2", good **$143**

Plumb bob. Turnip, gunmetal, steel point, 6 1/2", good **$105**

Plumb bob. G.J. Tyte, 1890, engraved on body and cap screw, brass ball, steel point, 4 3/4", good+ **$181**

Plumb bobs. Graduated set, sizes from 00 to 7, brass, steel points, fine **$143**

Plumb bobs. Stanley, reel, set of three, Nos. 1 and 2 in brass, No. 5 in iron, No. 1 unmarked early type and polished, larger two marked Stanley, good and better...**$352**

Plumb weight. Cast brass, 4 1/4", base diameter 1 1/8", good **$126**

Plummet lamp. Lamp and plumb bob combination for working in mines, fine+...**$1,650**

Plummet plumb bob. Owner made, hollow, screw cap, wood spool, good+ **$33**

Pry bar. Stanley No. 68B, beryllium, finish 99%, unused, fine **$55**

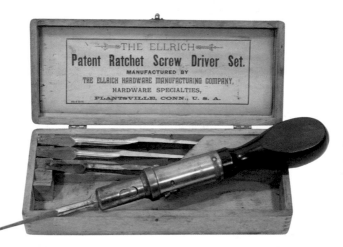

Ratchet screwdriver. Ellrich patent, four bits, original box, inside paper label, fine, $154.

Ratchet screwdriver. Ellrich patent, four bits, original box, inside paper label, fine..**$154**

Quarry man's tool. Crandall, iron, 24 points, wedge locked, good...**$99**

Rounders. J. Wanner, graduated set of nine, approximately 5/8" to 1 1/4", oak, good+................**$385**

Shoe measure. Stanley, measures shoe sizes to 13 and inches to 12, maple, fine, $440.

*Tool handle. Wooden brace-type brass chuck,
rosewood and brass, 19 bits including an uncommon
knife blade, walnut fitted box, good+, $412.*

Scale. Salter Letter Balance No. 11, brass dial and tray, repainted cast-iron body, good+...................................**$71**

Screwdrivers. Clark's best quality, handle, four bits, original fitted wood box, good label, good+............ **$192**

Shoe measure. Stanley, measures shoe sizes to 13 and inches to 12, maple, fine **$440**

Tool handle. Wooden brace-type brass chuck, rosewood and brass, 19 bits including an uncommon knife blade, walnut fitted box, good+... **$412**

Tool Chests
& Benches

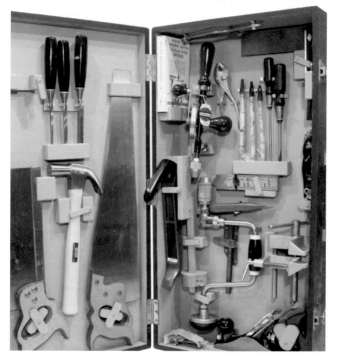

This section includes listings and illustrations of a number of chests that were crafted specifically to hold either a set of tools or a general collection of tools in general use in the past. Most of these chests were hand-crafted in wood and can range from fairly primitive pine examples to finely detailed and carefully crafted works of art built with pride by a craftsman of the past.

Tool chest. Dovetailed, covered tills front and back, two tool tills plus saw and plane tills, light wood w/ strong grain, strip of dark wood divides face of tills, 21" high, 36" wide, 21" deep, good, $110.

Carver's tool chest. Buck, 30 carving chisels in two fitted lift-out trays, many wider cuts, few narrow tools, storage area in bottom contains laminated mallet and book on carving, good+.. **$495**

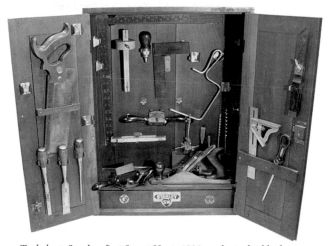

Tool chest. Stanley, first Sweet Hart, 1923, walnut, double doors, tray below, brass tags inside and out, about 21 original tools w/ V and first Sweet Hart logos, Disston dovetail saw marked Stanley, No. 65 3/4 gauge, No. 5 1/4 plane, three everlasting chisels, framing square, No. 80 scraper, No. 151 shave, only zigzag rule shows heavy use, good+ and better, $990.

Machinist's tool chest. H. Gerstner & Co., oak, 11 drawers and top till, outside finish 93%, good+...... **$242**

Machinist's tool chest. Able L. Reeves, walnut, four drawers w/ locking rod inside top tray, 21" wide, 14" deep, 13" high, good+... **$313**

Tool chest. Stanley, Sweet Hart, large size, sloping top, full of tools, two Everlasting chisels and Sweet Hart pliers, some tools probably original to box, full decal inside, good, $198.

Tool bench. E.W. Carpenter, Lancaster, "J. Souder" owner mark, head and side vises, tool till in back, drawer under bench, 8' 9" long, good, $770.

Tool bench. Hammacher, Schlemmer & Co., Doelger patent, July 28, 1896, oak, maple bench top and end vise, four drawers, trays, and tills, AM Tool Co. iron vise can be bolted on one end, no tools, much original finish, good+.. **$2,530**

Tool chest. Stanley, made in England, possibly 1970s, complete, nearly 30 new items, two still wrapped, fine **$242**

Tool chest. Dovetailed, light-colored wood w/ strong grain pattern, possibly lancewood, covered rear till, three sliding tills, 20" high, 36" wide, 24" deep, good **$154**

Tool chest. Used by W.H. Cox of Cox & Burdsfield Lumber, Minevera, Ohio, to store business records, owner name cast in letters on outside front, E missing in town name, double-top lid w/ storage on one side, ledge flip clips on other side lock behind wood lid, key, 12" deep, 21" long, 14" high, good+, $264.

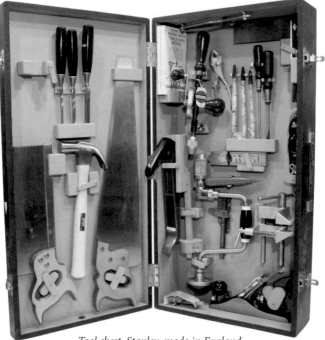

*Tool chest. Stanley, made in England,
possibly 1970s, complete, nearly 30 new
items, two still wrapped, fine, $242.*

*Tool chest. Stanley No. 851, 33 added tools, most
Stanley, Sweet Hart pliers, No. 610 pistol-grip drill,
door decal on box 100%, finish 97%, good, $440.*

Tool chest. Used by W.H. Cox of Cox & Burdsfield
Lumber, Minevera, Ohio, to store business records,
owner name cast in letters on outside front, E missing in
town name, double-top lid w/ storage on one side, ledge
flip clips on other side lock behind wood lid, key, 12"
deep, 21" long, 14" high, good+ **$264**

Tool chest. Stanley, first Sweet Hart, 1923, walnut,
double doors, tray below, brass tags inside and out,

Tool chest. Stanley No. 951, roll-top box,
27 probably original tools, fine, $660.

Tool chest. Dovetailed, inlaid lid and tills, at least 10 different woods in block optic pattern, four burl panels at corners of lid, five tills, top ones have covers in diamond pattern of light and dark wood, 20" high, 37" long, 21" deep, good+, $2,475.

about 21 original tools w/ V and first Sweet Hart logos, Disston dovetail saw marked Stanley, No. 65 3/4 gauge, No. 5 1/4 plane, three everlasting chisels, framing square, No. 80 scraper, No. 151 shave, only zigzag rule shows heavy use, good+ and better............................ **$990**

Tool chest. Stanley No. 850, oak, roll-top front, decal 40%, drawer, all clips, no tools, much original finish, fine **$154**

Tool chest. Stanley No. 850, oak, roll-top front, decal 65%, missing some hangers, finish clean and original, fine **$143**

Tool chest. Stanley No. 850, c. 1925, oak, dark stain, roll-top front, Stanley Tools decal on inside, 25" wide, 31" high, fine **$352**

Tool chest. Stanley, Sweet Hart, large size, sloping top, full of tools, two Everlasting chisels and Sweet Hart pliers, some tools probably original to box, full decal inside, good.. **$198**

Tool chest. Stanley No. 852, Sweet Hart, walnut, all tools including No. 204 in-out zigzag and odd jobs w/ rule and pliers, all but small items marked Sweet Hart, brass tags on chest in and out, good and better **$935**

Tool chest. Stanley No. 862, Sweet Hart, oak, original tools, key, good+ **$770**

Tool till. "D.L.", hinged cover inlaid w/ crossed handsaws and brass initials, blind dovetails, four or more different woods, good... **$99**

Tool tote. Stanley No. 888, sloping-lift top lids, brass tag on top, decal inside, 10 tools, No. 923 10" brace, No. 672 vise, No. 77 gauge, mitre square, No. 110 block plane, No. 106 zigzag, fine...**$715**

Tool tote. Old green paint, battered sides and ends, 33", good **$38**

Tool board. Twenty Stanley tools for 1954 Soap Box Derby mounted on framed board, good, $247

*Tool tote. Stanley No. 888, sloping-lift top lids,
brass tag on top, decal inside, 10 tools, No. 923 10"
brace, No. 672 vise, No. 77 gauge, mitre square,
No. 110 block plane, No. 106 zigzag, fine, $715.*

Clubs and Organizations

National Groups

Early American Industries Asso. Inc.
Elton W. Hall, Executive Director
167 Bakerville Road
South Dartmouth, MA 02748-4198
eaiainfo.org

Mid-West Tool Collectors Asso.
www.mwtca.org

Missouri Valley Wrench Club
Mala McGhee, Secretary-Treasurer
8291 Highway 39
Hollandale, WI 53544-9949
www.mvwc.org

The Tool Group of Canada
thetoolgroupofcanada.com/

Regional Groups

Antique Tools & Trades in Connecticut
Harry Audley
61 Hawthorne
Fairfield, CT 06825
(203) 371-4701
www.attic-us.org

CRAFTS of New Jersey
c/o Jim Bode
P.O. Box 372
Claverack, NY 12513
www.craftsofnj.org

Long Island Antique Tool Collectors Association
Ray Wisnieski
36 Spinner Lane
Commack, NY 11725
www.liatca.org

New England Tool Collectors Asso.
Avrum Silverman, Treasurer
69 Edgemore Avenue
Wellesley, MA 02482

Ohio Tool Collectors Association
Wayne Michael
226 Mills Place
New Lebanon, OH 45345
www.geocities.com/ohio_tool

Pacific Northwest Tool Collectors
Bill Racine
12780 SW 231st Place
Hillsboro, OR 97123
(503) 628-1488
www.tooltimer.com/PNTC.htm

PAST Tool Collectors
www.pasttools.org

**Potomac Antique Tools
and Industries Association**
www.patinatools.org

Rocky Mountain Tool Collector
Grace Goss
229 SE 22 St.
Loveland, CO 80537
www.rmtc.org

Southwest Tool Collectors Asso.
Carl Blair
712 S. Linden Ct. Ln.
Mustang, OK 73064-4140
www.swtca.org

Three Rivers Tool Collectors Asso.
Bob Kaltenhauser
(724) 352-1860

**Western New York Antique Tool
  Collectors Association**
Chuck Wirtenson
(315) 363-7682
wnyatca.org

Glossary

Adze Eye: The socket that a handle fits into. Generally applies to hammers and refers to a square hole in the head of the hammer that receives the handle.

Angle Bisector: A device that with gears or other linkage determines the exact half of an angle.

Architect's Rule: A rule with scales for reading architectural plans. Most often these rules have bevel edges to allow the rule's markings to rest directly on the surface of the paper, thereby improving the accuracy of the reading.

Back Saw: A saw with a heavy metal strip along the top of the blade. The strip was intended to keep the saw straight and avoid kinking. Backs can be brass or steel.

Bailey Plane: An early plane manufactured by Leonard Bailey. Not to be confused with Stanley planes marked "Bailey" after his death in 1905.

Beam Drill: A tool used to bore holes in timber framing, shipbuilding and other heavy work. The user sits on the base holding the tool down and with hand over hand motion bores the hole.

Bed Rock: A brand of Stanley planes that were offered from about 1895 to World War II. The Bed Rocks were offered only as bench planes and were heavier and of better construction than the regular Stanley line.

Beech: A light tan wood that has a uniform grain pattern. The most common wood used to make planes.

Bench Plane: The basic hand plane of all wood working trades. Bench planes have flat bottoms and cutters that do not extend to the edge of the plane. Length can range from 5" to 30" or more. Smaller sizes are smoothers, jacks are about 14", fore planes are 18", and jointers are more than 20" or so.

Bevel gauge, bevel or bevel square: A square that can be set to various angles. Used to lay out matching angles.

Bit Brace: A tool used to drill holes. The brace has a crank design, as opposed to the geared drives found on hand drills.

Board scale, rule or caliper: A measuring device with tables to determine the board feet of lumber in a board.

Bone: A white material that often has a strong grain pattern. Can be from many sources, but the most desirable is whalebone.

Bow Drill: A hand drill that uses a bow to power the drill bit. Often quite fancy, these tools were widely used in instrument making. Generally limited to making smaller holes.

Bow Saw: A group of saws that have a frame that pivots in the middle and is tensioned on the side opposite the blade. Many trades used this type of saw and the saw can be found in all shapes and sizes.

Boxwood: A light, tea-colored wood from Turkey. Most widely used in folding rules.

Breast Drill: A drill similar to a hand drill but with a pad at the top the user can lean on to apply additional pressure.

Butt gauge: A gauge used to lay out mortises for hinges. Hinges are often referred to as butts.

Chuteboard (Shootboard): A planing device that holds the work at a given angle and guides the plane during cutting. Often these were manufactured with the plane and board as a single unit.

Caliper and caliper rules: Measuring devices that can be adjusted to measure width, thickness or similar distances.

Circular Plane: A wood or metal plane that has a round bottom that can be adjusted to cut differing radius circles.

Cocobolo: A reddish wood from the rosewood family. Found most often on older bit braces.

Compass Plane: A wooden plane with a bottom that curves from the front to back. Used to cut a round surface, as in round top windows.

Cooper: A tradesman who makes wooden containers, such as barrels, buckets, firkins, and churns.

Core Box Plane: A plane used by pattern maker's to cut round cores.

Cranked Chisel: A chisel with the blade offset from the handle. These tools allow the user to hold the chisel flat against the work with his hand well above the surface.

Crosscut Saw: A saw with teeth designed to cut across the grain of the wood. Also refers to a large lumberman's saw used to cut timber.

Dado Plane: A dado plane is a rabbet plane with a skew or angled cutter. Dados are designed to cut across grain, and have a nicker to score the wood ahead of the blade.

Draw Shave: An edged tool with handles at the ends of the blade. A roughing out tool that can cut off a lot of material in a hurry, and is used by drawing the tool towards the user.

Ebony: A heavy black wood from central Africa. Traditional Gabon ebony was jet black and without grain.

Extension Rule: A measuring device that consists of two separate rules that slide to increase the overall length rule. Most examples have scales that measure the total length of the two rules.

Folding Rule: A rule that is made of a few sections and can be folded up. Eight sections are about the most found. Can be of many materials, but boxwood and ivory are the most common.

Fore Plane: A bench plane about 18" in length.

Fret Saw: A saw with a deep throat for sawing thin veneer-like materials.

Fruitwood: A heavy wood with little grain that ranges in color from light tea color to dark brown. Can come from many different fruit bearing trees, with apple being the most common.

German Silver: A bronze-type metal that has a silver finish and takes a polish that is similar to silver but not as bright.

Goosewing Ax: An early style of ax that is shaped like a goose's wing. Can be found with both square and round backs. These axes were originally from Europe and were made well into the 20th century. The Pennsylvania Dutch brought the style to America and made goosewing axes in the 18th and early 19th century.

Gunmetal: A bronze-like metal between brass and true bronze. Used in many English tools and some American. Color varies considerably but generally deep yellow and more red than brass.

Hand Drill: A tool used for drilling holes. Most often the drill is turned with gears. Hand drills have a handle that can be gripped with one hand. Breast drills have a wide flat pad that the user can lean on.

Handwrought: Hand-worked metal shaped and finished by hand. Handwrought does not mean poor workmanship, and the finer, more valuable pieces are higher quality than any machine-made item could ever be.

Hewing Ax: An ax sharpened on one side of the blade and used for hewing (flattening) round timbers. These axes are large, with edges of 10" or more.

Inclinometer: A leveling device that can measure the angle that a surface deviates from the level or plumb. Comes in many forms and some are quite complex. Most also function as a level.

Ivory: A white material derived primarily from elephant tusks.

Jack Plane: A bench plane about 14 inches long.

Japanning: A finish applied to tools. Originally, a mixture of lacquer and Japan colors, hence the name. On tools it is usually black, but occasionally red.

Jointer Fence: A device that can be attached to the side of a plane and used to guide the plane at a pre-determined angle.

Jointer Plane: A bench plane about 22 inches long.

Keyhole Saw: A small saw with a long tapered blade used for cutting angles, as in a keyhole.

Log scale, rule or caliper: A measuring device with tables to determine the board feet of lumber that can be sawn from a log.

Mahogany: A reddish wood lighter in weight than many of the other woods found in tools. Often has a considerable grain pattern.

Marking Gauge: A gauge with a sliding head and fixed marking points used to scratch layout lines a fixed distance from an edge. The mortise gauge looks similar but has two or more adjustable points. Can be made of many different woods and materials.

Match Plane: A plane designed to cut tongue-and-groove joints. Can be a set of two matching planes or a single plane that cuts both the tongue and groove.

Miller's Patent: Refers to several patents issued to Charles Miller of the Stanley Rule and Level Co. Patents cover several designs, the most common being the plow planes.

Mitre: A 45-degree wood joint.

Mitre Plane: A plane designed to cut across grain, as on a mitred edge. Cutter is set at a low angle, and the body is often lower and longer than a smooth plane.

Molding Plane: A plane designed to cut a decorative design. Can be single or simple mold, or a complex molder made of two or more simple molds.

Mortise Gauge: A marking gauge with two points set a certain distance apart for laying out two parallel lines a fixed distance from an edge. Mortise gauges can have fixed or adjustable points. The adjustments and materials used in construction are many.

Nicker: A knife-like blade found on planes. The blade is set at the edge of the plane to cut the wood ahead of the cutter and prevent tear out.

Original Box: The box the tool was sold in when new. Original boxes are quite rare and can add value to the item.

Pad Saw: A saw having a small handle with a narrow blade passing through the center of the handle. Used like a keyhole saw.

Panel Raiser: A plane designed to cut the edge of raised panels. Raised panels are most often found in doors and some furniture panels.

Patent: A license to manufacture a tool or item of the patentee's original design. Patents started in 1795 and are still issued today. A patent is good for 17 years and can be renewed for an additional 17 years. The U.S. Patent Office oversees the issuing of patents.

Patent Applied For: For up to one year before a patent is issued, an inventor is allowed to manufacture and sell his idea. The "patent applied for" status gives the same protection as the patent. The words are often found on tools and are abbreviated in many different ways.

Patent Model: A small detail model of an item described in a patent application. In the early years, patent models were required with the patent application. For a model to be considered a patent model it must have documentation.

Pattern Maker's Plane: A plane designed to cut a concave groove in a surface. Often found with sets of blades and bottoms that can be interchanged to cut varying radiuses.

Pit Saw: A two-man saw used to rip logs into lumber. One man stood below the log in a pit; hence, the name.

Pitch Level: A specific type of inclinometer that measures the amount of pitch. Often used by pipe layers; therefore, the scales read in inches of pitch per foot.

Plating: Nickel-plating, as opposed to chrome plating.

Plow Plane: A plane designed to cut a groove in the surface of a board. Most often has an adjustable fence and varying width cutters.

Plumb Bob: A pointed weight that can be hung on a string to determine a vertical, or plumb, line.

Plumb Weight: Similar to the plumb bob but with a flat bottom, rather than a point. Used when the string is the line of reference not the point of the bob.

Point-of-Sale Display: An often fancy display rack or stand used to sell an item in a hardware store.

Proof Rule: A slide rule with tables to calculate the proof of alcohol. Primarily customs agents used these.

Pump Drill: A hand drill that uses a pumping action to rotate the bit. Early examples had stone flywheels, while later ones use brass and other materials. Similar drills that use cords or chains with return springs to power the bit are occasionally encountered.

Rabbet Plane: Rabbet planes are designed to cut to the very edge of the plane. The cutter, therefore, extends to one or both edges of the plane. Rabbets can be found from a couple of inches long to over 24 inches long.

Rip Saw: A saw with teeth designed to cut with the grain of the wood.

Rope Rule or Caliper: A special rule for measuring rope and wire. Most often, they have a caliper to measure the diameter, and tables to determine such things as pounds per foot, strength, etc.

Rosewood: A reddish wood with black flecks that is the wood of choice for tool handles and parts.

Router: A plane-like tool with a single cutter design to cut the bottom of a groove.

Sash: A window, or a tool, such as a sash plane, used to make windows.

Scraper: A tool with a blade held nearly vertical and that cuts with a scraping action. Can be found in many forms and designs.

Scrub Plane: A plane for rough cutting wood quickly. Cutter has a slightly round edge and can remove a lot of material quickly.

Sector Rule: A thin, flat rule with rows of tables used for mathematical calculations. Often about 6 inches long and made of ivory.

Sewing Rule: A small advertising rule that was often a store giveaway. The most common length is 6". Can be made from wood, paper, celluloid and other inexpensive materials.

Ship Carpenter's or Shipwright's Bevel: A rule with a blade that folds out of the ends of the rule. The blade can be set at any angle to the body of the rule. Most of these rules have two brass blades, one slightly longer than the other.

Shoe Rule: A caliper rule made especially for the shoe salesman. The caliper slides to determine the length of the foot, and tables indicate shoe size. Often found with folding caliper jaws so the rule fits neatly into the salesman's pocket.

Side Ax: An ax that is sharpened on only one side of the blade. Used by numerous trades, these axes are encountered in many shapes and forms. Larger ones are often referred to as hewing axes.

Side Rabbet: A plane designed to cut the edge of a groove.

Sighting Level: A level that can be used to set a level line some distance from the user. Some designs use sights on top of or in the body of the level; other designs incorporate lenses and optics for better accuracy.

Slip Stick: Another name for an extension rule. The term "slip stick" tends to refer to an extension rule intended just for inside measure, as in a slip stick for measuring wood screens.

Slitting Gauge: A marking gauge with a knife in place of the point. Used to cut pieces of wood from a board.

Smooth Plane: A bench plane about 9 inches long.

Smoother: A smooth plane.

Spoke Shave: An edged tool with blade mounted between two handles. The blade is often held in place in a manner similar to that used on planes. Spoke shaves are like drawknives but are used for finer cuts.

Stair Saw: A small saw used to cut tread housing in stair construction. Most have a short blade and an adjustment to control depth of cut.

Sweet Hart: A trademark used by Stanley in the 1920s. The design consists of a heart with the word "Stanley" above. The Sweet Hart honored William Hart, a longtime Stanley employee.

Tape Rule: A metal rule that can be pulled out of a case. The tape rule replaced the folding rule starting in the 1930s.

Tee Rabbet Plane: A rabbet plane with a sole wider than the body of the plane. From the end the plane will resemble an inverted T.

Tongueing & Grooving Plane: Another name for match planes.

Toothing Plane: A plane with a notched blade that is nearly vertical. Used to scrape fine grooves in a surface for better gluing, as in veneer work.

Trammels: Points slide along a beam to measure or lay out distances or arches. Found in many different materials and forms.

Transitional or Wooden Bottom Plane: A plane with a wooden bottom and metal top section that holds the cutter. Generally marketed as a second-line tool.

Traveler: A wheel with a handle designed to measure distance around a circle. Wheel makers often used travelers to measure the distance around a wheel.

Try Square: A common square used by many trades. Can be found in many materials, but the rosewood handle with steel blade is the most common.

Wantage Rod: A device used to measure how much liquid is required to fill a vessel that is not completely empty.

Bibliography

Blanchard, Clarence. *Stanley Little Big Book, A Comprehensive Pocket Price Guide for Planes*. Pownal, Maine: published by the author, 2006.

_____. *Stanley Little Big Book, A Comprehensive Pocket Price Guide for Rules, Levels & Other Stanley Tools*. Pownal, Maine: published by the author, 2007.

Batcheller, Millton H., Jr. *American Marking Gauges*. Plainville, Mass.: published by the author, 2000.

Butterworth, Dale & Tom Whalen. *From Logs to Lumber, A History of People & Rule Making in New England*. Marshfield Hill, Mass.: Agicook Press, 2007.

Devitt, Jack. *Ohio Toolmakers and Their Tools*. Anderson, S.C: Tavenner Publishing Co., 2000.

_____. *Indiana Toolmakers and Their Tools*. Ann Arbor, Mich.: Sheridan Books Inc., 2002.

Goodman, W.L. *British Planemaker's from 1700*, 3rd Edition. Mendham, N.J.: Astragal Press, 1993.

Kebabian, Paul. *American Woodworking Tools*. Boston: New York Graphic Society, 1978.

Lamond, Thomas. *Manufactured and Patented Spokeshaves & Similar Tools*. Lynbrook, N.Y.: published by the author, 1997.

Page, Herb. *The Brothers Coes and their Legacy of Wrenches*. Davenport, Iowa: Sunset Mercantile Enterprises, 2004.

Pollak, Emil & Martyl. *A Guide to the Makers of American Wooden Planes*, 4th Edition. Mendham, N.J.: Astragal Press, 2001.

Sellens, Alvin. T*he Stanley Plane, A History and Descriptive Inventory*. Augusta, Kan., 1975.

Smith, Roger K. *Patent Transitional & Metallic Planes in America, 1827-1927*, Volume 1. Lancaster, Mass.: North Village Publishing Co., 1981.

_____. *Patent Transitional & Metallic Planes in America, 1827-1927*, Volume 2. Athol, Mass.: published by the author, 1992.

Stanley, Philip E. *Boxwood & Ivory Stanley Traditional Rules, 1855-1975*. Westborough, Mass.: Stanley Publishing Co., 1984.

A

adzes,
  bowl, 103, 106
  combination, 109
  hand, 111-112
apple parer, 450
apple peeler, 450
augers, 84, 87
  axes, 104, 106-107
  boarding, 106
  cooper's, 109
  felling, 110
  goose-wing, 110-112
  hewing, 112
  mast, 113
  miner's track, 113
  mortise, 113
  pick, 113
  presentation, 114
  shipbuilder's, 115
  side, 115
  socket, 116
ax heads, 104, 114

B

beaders, 450-451, 460
bellows, 451-452
bench, tool, 477
bevels,
  double, 391-393
  protractor, 376
  ship carpenter's, 414
  sliding T, 414
  square, 376

blind nailing tool, 451
board stick, 378
boiler inspector's rule, 379
bolt cutter, 106
bookbinder's creasers, 453
books, 61
braces, 69-79, 85
  blacksmith's, 67
  cage-head, 81
  chair maker's, 81-82, 84
  framed, 82-84, 88
  piano maker's, 86
  surgeon's, 84, 87, 89
  wagon maker's, 89
  washer cutting, 89-90
  wooden, 91-92
brad awls, 453

C

calipers, 385- 386
  double, 395
  gunner's, 396, 400
  head, 401
  ivory, 401
  lady's leg, 408
  log, 408
  outside, 411
  storekeeper's, 416
canes,
  board, 376, 452-453
  log, 408
  lumber, 462
carving tools, 107
catalogs, 61-64